EVERY COCKTAIL HAS A TWIST

Also by Carey Jones and John McCarthy:

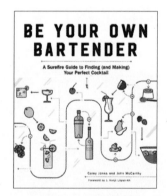

Be Your Own Bartender:
A Surefire Guide to Finding (and Making) Your Perfect Cocktail

Master 25 Classic Drinks and
Craft More Than 200 Variations

EVERY COCKTAIL HAS A TWIST

CAREY JONES AND JOHN McCARTHY

PHOTOGRAPHY BY RACHEL WEILL

Countryman Press

An Imprint of W. W. Norton & Company
Celebrating a Century of Independent Publishing

Illustration credits: Page 3, 20, 42, 50, 74, 82, 90, 104, 113, 124, 134, 144, 153, 176, 185, 194, 202, 212, 222, 229, 236, 244: iStockPhoto.com / Inna Miller; page 32, 202: iStockPhoto.com / discan; page 64: iStock-Photo.com / Tatiana Pankova; page 98: iStockPhoto.com / Olena Dumanchuk; page 98: iStockPhoto.com / ONYXprj; page 144, 164: iStockPhoto.com / OrlyDesign; page 202: iStockPhoto.com / mayalis

For information about permission to reproduce selections from this book, write to
Permissions, Countryman Press, 500 Fifth Avenue, New York, NY 10110

For information about special discounts for bulk purchases, please contact
W. W. Norton Special Sales at specialsales@wwnorton.com or 800-233-4830

Manufacturing through Asia Pacific Offset
Book design by Allison Chi
Production manager: Devon Zahn

Countryman Press
www.countrymanpress.com

An imprint of W. W. Norton & Company, Inc.
500 Fifth Avenue, New York, NY 10110
www.wwnorton.com

978-1-68268-729-1 (pbk)

10 9 8 7 6 5 4 3 2 1

We raise our glasses to home bartenders everywhere.

CONTENTS

INTRODUCTION

CRAFT COCKTAILS, you can find them everywhere. Far beyond dedicated cocktail bars—at restaurants, special events, online—creative drinks have become commonplace. But no matter how esoteric some drinks may appear, we all come back to the standards, the drinks we know and love: classic cocktails, to be sure, but not the kind that primarily reside as recipes in pre-Prohibition books or in the depths of solemn mixologists' brains.

What do most of us drink? Brunch drinks, such as the Bloody Mary and Sangria. Winter staples, including an Eggnog or a Hot Toddy. Juleps for Derby Day; Pimm's Cups for a summer garden party; vacation-worthy Mojitos and Mai Tais; and of course Manhattans and Martinis when the occasion strikes.

Not only standbys in their own right, classic drinks give us an amazing jumping-off point to the entire world of cocktails. So many drinks at modern cocktail bars fundamentally riff on the classics. Once you've mastered your Old-Fashioned technique, try one with rye and maple syrup or one with Scotch and St-Germain. Like a Moscow Mule? You might love it with tart cherry or smoky mezcal. You can create a spritz with literally dozens of bottles beyond Aperol.

In this book, we'll teach you to make 25 staple drinks: pre-Prohibition classics such as the Sazerac and French 75, perennial favorites including the Margarita and Daiquirí, and relative newcomers such as the Espresso Martini. We'll look at each drink's history, provide tips on technique, and show you how to make a stellar version at home. Then we'll take you through half a dozen or more variations of each, which involve all manner of novel spirits, liqueurs, or produce that always preserve the essential character of the drink you know and love.

Whether you don't own a muddler or if you have 200 bottles in your collection, this book is for you, the home bartender. We'll discuss fundamental ways to make your home drinks better. Remembering a few cardinal rules will take you a long way. But like anyone, we love a good shortcut, too. Whizzing up Eggnog in a blender? A Sangria that doesn't need overnight steeping? We're all for it. This book offers elegant gin Martinis and dirty vodka variations, beer-topped Margaritas and cleverly obscure Sazerac riffs. Some recipes are crowd pleasers, some are for the cocktail geeks—we love it all.

We're John McCarthy and Carey Jones, a husband-wife cocktail team. A mixologist by trade, John has created cocktail programs for more than a dozen bars, restaurants, and hotels in New York and beyond. Carey has written about food, travel, and spirits for 15 years. Together, we've spent more than a decade writing about cocktails for leading publications, including *Food & Wine* and *Saveur*; developing recipes for major spirits brands; and teaching cocktail classes to experienced bartenders and novices alike.

In our first book, *Be Your Own Bartender,* we took a booze-your-own-adventure approach to the world of modern cocktails, helping you find the best drink for any mood or occasion with the help of some handy flowcharts. For this book, we're taking the same spirit of exploration but grounding it squarely in the classics. You no doubt have a favorite drink or two—or few. Let's make them great and keep expanding your horizons, too.

HOW WE NAME OUR COCKTAILS

Many classic cocktails don't have a single definitive recipe. Bartenders argue endlessly about the ratio of lime to rum in a Daiquirí, or how many dashes of bitters should go in a Sazerac. Like everyone else, we have our opinions! When we designate a recipe a "Classic" in this book, it means it's more-or-less an indisputable recipe—that is, it's made with the same spec the world over, such as the Aperol Spritz. We consider drinks designated "Our Classic" as the best way to make them. There are many ways to make a Martini, for instance, but we're giving you our preferred ratios. Where you can make a drink in multiple ways, we'll acknowledge that, too. Such drinks include the build-in-a-glass Simplest Mojito and the Cocktail Mojito, shaken and strained.

THE BASICS

Basic bartending gear, which is available at any kitchen store, is inexpensive and long-lasting. Don't get started without the proper equipment.

ESSENTIAL TOOLS

Barspoon
A standard spoon is too short for the task, so this is essential for all stirred drinks.

Jigger
Your jigger or set of jiggers should measure in ¼ ounce, ½ ounce, ¾ ounce, 1 ounce, and ideally 1½ and 2 ounce increments for spirits, juices, and syrups.

Shaker
Use this tool for all cocktails shaken with ice—and as a rule: any drink with citrus juice. A cobbler shaker (cap and built-in strainer) or a Boston shaker (pint glass and metal tin) both work, but a set of tins is the most practical and durable, and metal won't shatter.

Strainer
A Hawthorne strainer, with a metal spiral around the edge and prongs to hold it tight to the shaker, is standard to strain a cocktail into its serving vessel.

RECOMMENDED

Citrus Juicer
Fresh juice is essential to many cocktails. A two-handled squeezer is effective and inexpensive. A reamer does the job, too, but requires a bit more work to strain out the seeds.

Citrus Peeler
A knife will work, but a straight or Y-shaped peeler is a better tool for cutting wide strips of citrus peel for a twist.

Ice Molds
Silicone ice molds yield attractive, square cubes. We like 1¼-inch cubes for shaking, stirring, and serving; and 2-inch cubes when you want one large cube (also known as "the rock") for a stirred drink like an

Old-Fashioned or Negroni. You can find silicone molds at most kitchen stores or online.

Fine Mesh Strainer
"Double straining" (or "fine straining") refers to the process of straining a drink through a fine mesh strainer, as well as the shaker's own strainer. When using a second strainer, you're aiming to catch small bits of fruit seeds, ice chips, or mint flecks.

Julep Strainer
This round strainer fits in a mixing glass to strain stirred drinks. Ironically, it's not used for making Juleps.

Mixing Glass
You can stir Martinis, Manhattans, and the like in a shaking tin, but a proper mixing glass looks far more elegant.

Muddler
Use one of these to break up ingredients such as ginger, cucumber, or berries right in the shaker.

NICE TO HAVE

Blender
Who doesn't want a frozen drink on a hot day?

Cocktail Picks
Certain garnishes just look better on small skewers. You can purchase inexpensive, disposable bamboo ones or metal picks for a dash of elegance.

Juice Extractor
It's much easier and quicker to make ginger juice, cucumber juice, even Sugar Snap Pea Juice (page 260) with a juice extractor.

Ice Bag and Mallet
The best low-tech way to crush ice—and the most satisfying way, especially if you have some frustration to exorcise—is to fill a canvas bag with ice and whack it with a mallet. Bar outfitters sell it under a particular name: Lewis bag.

GLASSWARE
In rough order of importance.

Rocks Glass
A short tumbler used for all kinds of sours, stirred drinks, and more. A single rocks glass, which can hold as few as 6 ounces,

may be too small for larger cocktails, so go for a double rocks glass, which generally holds about 10 to 12 ounces.

Coupe

This stemmed glass with a shallow bowl is the classic presentation for any drink served "up," meaning without ice. Some cocktails, such as the Margarita or the Whiskey Sour, can be served either up or on the rocks, as the drinker prefers. The versatile coupe also can be used for Champagne or Martinis.

Collins

A tall, slim tumbler is the preferred glass for the eponymous Tom Collins, as well as highballs, such as a gin and tonic, sodas, and other nonalcoholic drinks. (The Highball, any two-ingredient mixed drink, consists of a spirit plus a usually carbonated mixer. The name comes from a railroad signaling device that indicated fast speed, which describes how quickly you can make the drink.)

Wine Glass

This standard, long-stemmed glass works best for spritzes and the like.

Flute

A tall, narrow, stemmed glass is the classic choice for Champagne, other sparkling wines, and some sparkling cocktails.

Pint Glass

This tall, wide glass is standard for serving beer and also proves useful for beer cocktails or larger nonalcoholic drinks.

SPECIALTY VESSELS

Copper Mug

This is the vessel of choice for a Moscow Mule, though a Collins glass or double rocks glass will work, as well.

Julep Cup

A large double rocks glass can accommodate a Mint Julep, but the classic silver mug is traditional and keeps your drink frostier longer.

Martini Glass

Based on size and aesthetics, a coupe is our choice for Martinis, but if you prefer this classic V-shaped glass, go for it.

TECHNIQUES

The essential skills of bartending aren't complicated, but proper attention to detail will take you a long way. In rough order of importance:

Shaking a Drink

As a rule of thumb, any drink with fresh citrus juice, including the Daiquirí or Whiskey Sour, needs shaking. Any drink with cream or egg does, too. Shaking a drink unifies the ingredients, aerates them, chills them, and provides proper dilution. It takes you from "liquids poured together" to a cocktail.

If using shaking tins, combine all liquid ingredients in the smaller tin. Fill the larger tin about two-thirds full of ice. Pour the liquid from the small tin into the large one, nestle the small tin into the large one,

then pound firmly to form a watertight seal. If you're using a cobbler shaker, which has a built-in strainer and cap, combine all liquids in the tin, then fill it about two-thirds full of ice, using one hand to prevent splashing, and seal. With one hand on each tin or one hand on the cobbler top, shake *hard*. You're imbuing the cocktail with life, pulling it all together, so put your heart into it! You want to hear and feel the ice flying back and forth inside, from one end of the shaker to the other. After 15 seconds of hard shaking, the tins will feel frosty. Unseal them, fit your strainer into the tin, and strain into the serving glass.

Stirring a Drink

If a drink contains no juice, cream, or eggs, you usually stir it, and stirring it long enough is essential. An under-stirred Martini or Manhattan will taste harsh and boozy. A perfectly stirred one, despite its potency, will taste velvety smooth.

Combine the liquid ingredients in a mixing glass (or a shaking tin). Fill it approximately three-quarters full of ice, using an ice scoop and your other hand as a splash guard. For the professional bartender move, fill the glass with cracked cubes by cracking each ice cube *hard* with the back of a barspoon before carefully adding it to the mixing glass. Cracked cubes help chill the drink more thoroughly, and it's a great technique for drinks such as the Martini and Manhattan. With so few ingredients, every element should be perfect, including the ice.

With the back of the barspoon running smoothly around the interior wall of the mixing glass, stir for 30 seconds. It may feel like a long time, but you want some of the ice to melt and to chill the drink closer to 32°F. Then strain the drink into your chilled glass and enjoy.

Garnishing with a Twist

Colorful citrus twists look attractive and, when done properly, add quite a bit to flavor a drink. Twisting an orange peel atop a cocktail releases its oils in a light spray that coats the surface, bringing a burst of citrus flavor to your nose on first sip. You can do a decorative garnish with citrus in many ways. A channel knife, for example, will give you a long, skinny, decorative peel that looks beautiful but isn't as aromatic.

With a straight or Y-shaped peeler, cut a long slice of citrus peel, at least ¾ inch wide and at least 2 inches long (up to 3 or

4 inches for a large orange or grapefruit). You want to get the colored rind but *not* much of the white pith. If you like, you can trim the sides of the peel with a small knife so it looks more manicured. Leaving the edges rough is fine, too. It's just an aesthetic choice. In some cases—such as when serving a drink in a narrow flute or when a full twist might overwhelm a delicate cocktail—a drink might benefit from a little bit of citrus oil but not a full twist. In these cases, we call for a "round" of peel, a circle about 1 inch in diameter, for a smaller garnish.

Once you've made and poured your cocktail, it's time for the twist. With thumbs and fingers of both hands, hold the citrus peel by both edges over the glass, skin side down. Pull the edges upward and together to express those enticing oils. If it's a good peel, you'll see and smell it immediately. Then run the skin side of the twist around the rim of the glass, which further distributes the citrus oils. (Don't do this if you're using a glass with a salt or sugar rim, obviously.) Most cocktails call for presenting the peel in the glass, skin side up; in other cases, such as the Sazerac, the twist is just for flavor, so you'll discard the peel.

Garnishing with Herbs
Fresh mint, basil, and rosemary make attractive garnishes, but their purpose isn't solely ornamental. The aromatics of a garnish dramatically impact how a drink tastes, and herb garnishes, in particular, are all about aromatics. Keep a few points in mind when working with herbs. Use clean, attractive sprigs. You're giving this drink a lot of love and attention, so it should look as beautiful as possible. Before you add the herbs to your drink, wake them up by smacking them against your hand. Doing so breaks some of the plant's cells, releasing their essential oils and aromas. Give it a try. Sniff a basil leaf, clap it between your hands, and sniff again. See how much more potent it becomes? The more delicate the herb, the more lightly you should treat it. Pretty sprigs of mint and basil get a light tap. Give the more robust rosemary a big clap between your palms.

Muddle
In the cocktail world, muddling means using a blunt instrument—ideally, a purpose-built muddler—to extract the botanicals from a plant or to smash an ingredient. The premise is simple: You're breaking up the ingredient to release its flavor. Muddling mint for a Julep, for example, imparts that herb's dynamic flavor into the drink. Muddling a fruit or vegetable breaks it down, causing it to incorporate into a cocktail without the bother of a juicer or a blender.

Different ingredients require different muddling techniques. Generally speaking, the harder an ingredient, the harder the muddle. Tough and fibrous ginger, for instance, needs a good pounding; strawberries, less so. With delicate herbs, including mint or basil, too much muddling can turn them into a bitter, brown paste. If you need to muddle multiple ingredients, start with the hardest ones first, which can take the most punishment. In the case of a drink such as the Fancy Dress Pimm's (page 205), with multiple muddled ingredients, you'll start with the ginger. With something as hardy as ginger, think *smash.* With cucumber, *break up.* With berries, *squish,* and with basil or mint, think *massage.* All muddling but in different ways.

Chilling Glassware

When you serve a drink "on the rocks," meaning with ice, those cubes will keep your cocktail cold. But what about when you serve it "up" in a coupe or martini glass? The drink can warm quickly. The solution to keeping its temperature down where it belongs is by chilling your glassware. You have two ways to do this. If you have room in your freezer, pop the glass or glasses inside; even just two minutes will help. Ten or more minutes will achieve a properly cold glass. (We also invite you to join our club of eccentrics who store coupes in their freezer, just in case the Gimlet mood strikes.) Alternatively, fill your serving glass to the brim with ice cubes and cold water so it chills while you prepare the cocktail. Discard the ice water just before you pour.

Rimming A Glass

A salted or sugared rim is always optional, but it can add a fun, eye-catching element to a cocktail. We'll use salt in the instructions that follow, but the same technique

applies to sugars; flavored sugars, as for the South American Sidecar (page 232); flavored salts, as for the Outer Sunset (page 199) or Paloma Spritz (page 201); or other seasonings, such as the Tajín Clásico Seasoning rim for the Mezcal Maria (page 40) or Frozen Honeydew Margarita (page 133).

Rim your glass as the first step, before putting ice or any liquid in it. If you're making multiple cocktails, do all the rims first before starting on the drinks.

Into a small plate or saucer, sprinkle a shallow, even layer of kosher salt. (Coarse sea salt is too large, and iodized table salt is too fine.) Take a citrus wedge that corresponds to your drink: lime for anything with lime juice, including most Margaritas and Palomas, or lemon for Sidecars with lemon juice. Cut a small notch in the flesh of the fruit. Nestle that notch over the rim of the glass and rotate the glass, using the citrus juice to coat the outside of the rim. The more juice you apply, the farther down your salt rim can go.

For a light rim just around the top of the glass, invert the moistened glass and briefly dip it in the salt. For a thicker rim around the outside of the glass, place the glass at an angle into the salt and use more of a rolling motion.

A few notes: Salt on the inside rim of the glass will make your drink salty, so use a clean towel to wipe the interior carefully. Also, a half or three-quarter rim looks great if you want the effect of a salted rim but want a "clean" area of the glass to sip from.

EIGHT STEPS TO BETTER COCKTAILS

Following a few basic rules will take you far in bartending.

INVEST IN THE RIGHT BOTTLES.

Some people who first get into cocktails will stock their bars immediately, using a "one of everything!" approach that can cost a serious bit of money. We recommend taking it one drink at a time. If you're a Margarita fan, start with a good Tequila blanco, or mezcal if that's your thing, and a quality orange liqueur. More of a Manhattan drinker? Then go for rye or Bourbon and a good sweet vermouth. Build your bar from the drinks that you know you'll make and let it evolve organically.

KNOW WHAT TO REFRIGERATE.

Any wine-based product, including vermouth (sweet and dry), Sherry, and aperitifs such as Lillet or Cocchi Americano, should go in the refrigerator once opened. In the fridge, most will last at least a month—or a few—without any notable decline in quality, but they do go off much more quickly than spirits. If you don't use vermouth often, buy it in half bottles.

USE ONLY FRESH CITRUS JUICE.

We wish there were a shortcut for lemon and lime juice. We wish that shelf-stable bottled juices could compare, but they simply don't. So no neon squeeze bottles! Without freshly squeezed lemon or lime juice, your Margarita or French 75 will lack vibrancy and taste flat. If you can't squeeze the lime or lemon juice, choose another drink entirely rather than use bottled juice. We also recommend straining your juices through a fine mesh strainer after squeezing to remove the pulp. The absence of pulp creates cleaner cocktails and also helps the juice last longer in the fridge.

For other fruits, such as oranges and grapefruits, purchasing fresh-squeezed juice is an acceptable substitute for squeezing yourself. But that means the kind that the grocery store makes, not a brand name. Also strain them before using. You can buy other bottled juices, including pomegranate, cranberry, and tart cherry, as long as they contain *only* that fruit juice; so, for example, "100% pomegranate juice." Plenty of "juice cocktails" are cut with apple, grape, or pear juices, which you don't want.

DON'T SKIP THE SUGAR.

Sweetener is essential to virtually all cocktails. Yes, many cocktails out there can taste too sweet, but the recipes in this book produce cocktails that carefully balance a drink's tart, boozy, or bitter qualities with exactly the right amount of sugar, thereby binding all the cocktail's elements together. With rare exceptions, as noted in the recipe descriptions, we wouldn't call any of these cocktails sweet. Also, don't bother skipping the sweetener for calories' sake. Most cocktail calories lurk in the alcohol, anyway.

ICE IS AN INGREDIENT.

Some cocktails have few ingredients, but ice is virtually always one of them, so take it seriously. Make sure you have plenty to shake or stir. Don't use ice that's been sitting in your freezer for six months because it'll taste like the rest of what's in your freezer. Crushed ice behaves differently than cubes, which melt differently than one big "rock." Always use the right ice for the job.

NO WIMPY SHAKES OR SHORT STIRS.

Stirring or shaking a cocktail combines the ingredients, chills them properly, and contributes a small amount of melted water—around 1 ounce per drink—that functions as a hidden ingredient, bringing the cocktail to the proof you want. In a more abstract sense, the act of shaking or stirring is how you, the bartender, are pulling the cocktail together. Shake vigorously; stir for 30 seconds. The difference in how a cocktail tastes is dramatic.

GARNISH MATTERS.

You can skip a cocktail umbrella, sure, but most garnishes provide key aromatics as well as visual appeal. A bold bouquet of mint is essential to a Julep. A twist of orange creates a burst of citrus oils that enlivens an Old-Fashioned. Make sure your garnishes are fresh and attractive.

CHOOSE THE RIGHT DRINKS FOR PARTIES.

Batching, in bartender parlance, means making multiples of a drink ahead of time. Some drinks batch easily, others not so much. Any drink that requires muddling, for instance, isn't a great candidate to batch. We provide workarounds where possible, though. We've also called out the best drinks for batching with recipe variations and sidebars.

Cheers! Now, let's get to the drinks!

1.

APEROL SPRITZES

LIGHT · BUBBLY · BITTERSWEET

I'd like it . . .

Easy to make, eye-catching color, bright and bubbly—what's not to like? Over the last decade, the Aperol Spritz, a regional Italian drink, emerged from relative obscurity to become one of the most popular cocktails on the planet. Savvy promotion by Gruppo Campari, which acquired the brand in the early aughts, can take much of the credit. But it's clear that the world eagerly wanted a low-alcohol, easy-drinking sparkling cocktail, and on all those fronts the Aperol Spritz delivers.

The word *spritz* comes from the German *spritzen,* which means "to splash." In the mid-1800s, the first spritz drinks consisted of local wine with a splash of club soda to lighten them. In Italy, where every corner of the country had its own vermouths and bitter liqueurs, many local products found their way into spritzes. The people of and around Padua particularly enjoyed the Aperol Spritz, which was advertised as early as the 1950s. But only in recent years did its popularity go global.

It's a beach drink, a brunch drink, a day drink, ideal for any time when a cocktail feels like a bit of a cheeky indulgence. Because of its low ABV, you can enjoy a spritz or two without overdoing the alcohol. Another round? Why not? Gently bitter and altogether mild in character, with notes of orange, rhubarb, and vanilla, Aperol offers an easy gateway to the world of *aperitivi.* If you like Aperol, odds are you'll love the Select aperitivo from Venice or the juicy, ruby-red Cappelletti from Italy's alpine north, one of the oldest red bitters still in production. Spritzes don't have to be bitter, either. Limoncello, elderflower, cucumber—let's spritz it all!

BUY THESE BOTTLES

Prosecco classically goes into spritzes, but many brands taste very sweet. Cava, Spain's traditional sparkling wine, tastes drier and is just as affordable. Look for Codorniu Anna Cava Brut (all-white bottle) or Dibon (bright orange label). Another great, affordable option is French sparkling wine. Crémants, such as Crémant d'Alsace, Crémant de Bourgogne, and so on, designate wines made with the Champagne method that don't come from the Champagne region. Save your expensive Champagne for, well, drinking. If you prefer Prosecco, choose a drier brand, such as Mionetto.

CLASSIC APEROL SPRITZ

The classic recipe has a 3:2:1 ratio, which makes it easy to remember.

3 ounces sparkling wine

2 ounces Aperol

1 ounce club soda

1 orange slice for garnish

In a large wine glass filled halfway with ice, combine all the ingredients, adding the club soda last. Stir gently and briefly. Garnish with a thin half-moon slice of orange.

WHAT'S A SPRITZ?

Aperol has become so popular that a tendency has arisen these days to call anything bubbly in a wine glass a spritz, almost like that cringey 1990s practice of dubbing all drinks 'tinis. We're a little more circumscribed in how we use the name. A cocktail containing sparkling wine, citrus juice, and a spirit probably runs closer to a French 75 (page 84). Just bubbles and juice fall into the Mimosa-Bellini family. But sparkling wine with supporting aperitifs or liqueurs? That sounds like a spritz to us.

ALPINE ROSE SPRITZ

Either Lillet Rosé or Cappelletti tastes delicious as a spritz, but they drink even better together. Lillet's citrus notes and Cappelletti's bright red energy come together seamlessly. It looks and drinks like an Aperol Spritz but with a lot more going on, and everything's more fun with rosé involved.

3 ounces sparkling rosé

1 ounce Cappelletti

1 ounce Lillet Rosé

1 ounce club soda

1 lemon wheel for garnish

In a large wine glass filled halfway with ice, combine all the ingredients, adding the club soda last. Stir gently and briefly. Garnish with a thin lemon wheel.

SPRITZ ALLA FRESCA

Your first Aperol Spritz can taste delightful, but some people find that, after another round, they feel a bit heavy. This Spritz, named for the Italian word for "fresh" (not the soda!) is much drier. A little vodka cuts the Aperol's sweetness while upping the proof a bit, and Topo Chico—an aggressively carbonated sparkling water and a bartender favorite—keeps it all energetic.

2 ounces sparkling wine

1 ounce Aperol

1 ounce vodka

2 ounces grapefruit Topo Chico

1 grapefruit slice for garnish

In a large wine glass filled halfway with ice, combine all the ingredients, adding the Topo Chico last. Stir gently and briefly. Garnish with a thin half-moon slice of grapefruit.

NOTE: We love grapefruit Topo Chico in this drink, but the unflavored version works, too. You want the brand's bold, in-your-face bubbles.

VENETIAN SPRITZ

If you like Aperol, you'll love Select, the preferred aperitivo to enjoy while floating along the canals of Venice. It's worth seeking out a bottle; once you've tried this spritz, you'll be using it up in no time. The olive in this cocktail may seem unexpected, but it's a traditional garnish. Think of it as a little snack for your aperitivo hour.

3 ounces sparkling wine

2 ounces Select aperitivo

1 ounce club soda

1 orange slice for garnish

1 green olive for garnish

In a large wine glass filled halfway with ice, combine all the ingredients, adding the club soda last. Stir gently and briefly. Garnish with a thin slice of orange and a skewered green olive.

BATCH IT

Aperol Assembly Line

Spritzes make great party drinks. But if you try to make them ahead of time, you'll lose those all-important bubbles fast. Instead of using a pitcher or punch bowl, set up an assembly line. Chill your bubbles and club soda, line up your glasses, ice 'em all, then go down the line with each ingredient, ending with a quick stir and the garnish. Show off a little, stir with a flourish, and have someone record it!

Sorrento Spritz

SORRENTO SPRITZ

Don't mind us; we'll be sitting over here with a cheery lemon spritz, dreaming of the Amalfi Coast. Make one real quick and join us.

3 ounces sparkling wine

1 ounce limoncello

1 ounce St-Germain
elderflower liqueur

1 ounce club soda

1 lemon wheel for garnish

2 or 3 sprigs mint for garnish

In a large wine glass filled halfway with ice, combine all the ingredients, adding the club soda last. Stir gently and briefly. Garnish with the lemon wheel placed between the wine glass and the ice. Lightly tap the mint sprigs against your hand to release their fragrant oils and add them to the glass, as well.

LIMONCELLO

Packed into the luggage of many a traveler returning from Italy, limoncello liqueur comes from lemon peels that, generally, hail from the Amalfi Coast. Sipped on its own, it can taste quite sweet. It also can star in cocktails, contributing a vibrant citrus flavor. Either way, it always benefits from being served ice-cold. We're partial to Luxardo's limoncello.

SUNSET SPRITZ

Significantly more bitter than Aperol, Campari takes this spritz in a more intense direction, while the orange liqueur ups the proof. This spritz tastes a little more potent, a little more dynamic, while still remaining bright, citrusy, and easy to drink.

3 ounces sparkling wine

1 ounce Campari

1 ounce Cointreau

1 ounce club soda

1 orange slice for garnish

In a large wine glass filled halfway with ice, combine all the ingredients, adding the club soda last. Stir gently and briefly. Garnish with a thin half-moon slice of orange.

LO-FI SPRITZ

This compelling spritz is for cocktail nerds who don't mind hunting for a few exciting bottles. Lo-Fi Gentian Amaro is one of our favorite new products of the last decade. Rich and sophisticated, it presents layered flavors of ginger, spice, and citrus. Here, racy yellow Chartreuse backs it up. The deep purple color makes this spritz just as photogenic as one with Aperol.

3 ounces sparkling wine

1½ ounces Lo-Fi Gentian Amaro

½ ounce yellow Chartreuse

1 ounce club soda

3 lemon wheels for garnish

In a large wine glass filled halfway with ice, combine all the ingredients, adding the club soda last. Stir gently and briefly. Garnish with three thin lemon wheels.

BUY THIS BOTTLE

Lo-Fi Gentian Amaro

OUTLIER SPRITZ

You rarely see Pimm's outside a Pimm's Cup, which is a shame, since it's such a compelling liqueur. Instead of club soda, use Fever-Tree's excellent cucumber-flavored tonic, which echoes a Pimm's Cup's traditional cucumber garnish. We consider this drink a spritz for all seasons: sip it on a sailboat, at a mountain lodge, on your fire escape "balcony"—however you do.

2 ounces Pimm's No. 1

2 ounces sparkling wine

2 ounces Fever-Tree
   Cucumber Tonic Water

1 lime wedge for garnish

1 cucumber slice, cut
   diagonally, for garnish

In a large wine glass filled halfway with ice, combine all the ingredients, adding the tonic water last. Stir gently and briefly. Squeeze the lime wedge into the glass and drop it in. Also garnish with the slice of cucumber.

DIRTY MONTE

You've heard of a Dirty Martini; now meet the Dirty Spritz. In Venice, it's traditional to garnish a spritz with an olive and an orange slice. We took it a step further and brought half an ounce of olive brine into the drink itself. If you can find them, use Spanish martini olives marinated in vermouth. Amaro Montenegro's herbal side shines with the salinity of the brine. This spritz's time in the sun has arrived, and we hope you love it as much as we do.

3 ounces sparkling wine

1½ ounces Amaro
   Montenegro

½ ounce green olive brine

1 ounce club soda

1 orange slice for garnish

1 green olive for garnish

In a large wine glass filled halfway with ice, combine all the ingredients, adding the club soda last. Stir gently and briefly. Garnish with a thin half-moon slice of orange and an olive.

BUY THIS BOTTLE

Amaro Montenegro

Dirty Monte

MIX AND MATCH

Try any of the following in a spritz. Start with the standard formula: sparkling wine, bitter liqueur, sparkling water. Some of these liqueurs taste sweeter than others, so adjust to taste. We've provided recipes that include Campari, Cappelletti, and Lillet Rosé in combination with other bitter liqueurs, but try using them solo. When in doubt, an orange slice makes the best garnish.

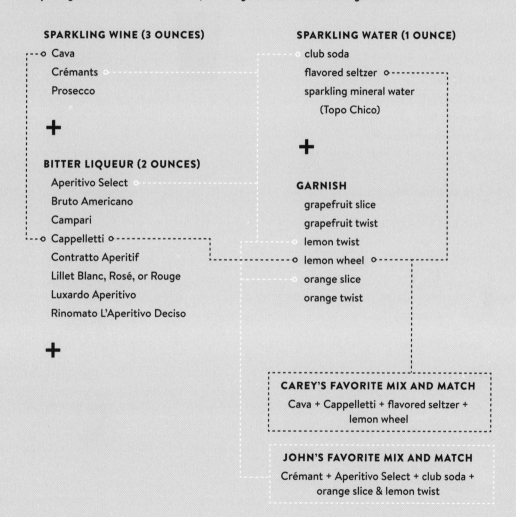

SPARKLING WINE (3 OUNCES)
- Cava
- Crémants
- Prosecco

+

BITTER LIQUEUR (2 OUNCES)
- Aperitivo Select
- Bruto Americano
- Campari
- Cappelletti
- Contratto Aperitif
- Lillet Blanc, Rosé, or Rouge
- Luxardo Aperitivo
- Rinomato L'Aperitivo Deciso

+

SPARKLING WATER (1 OUNCE)
- club soda
- flavored seltzer
- sparkling mineral water
  (Topo Chico)

+

GARNISH
- grapefruit slice
- grapefruit twist
- lemon twist
- lemon wheel
- orange slice
- orange twist

CAREY'S FAVORITE MIX AND MATCH
Cava + Cappelletti + flavored seltzer + lemon wheel

JOHN'S FAVORITE MIX AND MATCH
Crémant + Aperitivo Select + club soda + orange slice & lemon twist

2. ....o

BLOODY MARYS

SAVORY · SALTY · BRUNCHY

MIX IT UP

One Bloody Mary . . .

It's zesty, spicy, and sipped usually in daylight hours. A cocktail outlier in every way, the Bloody Mary is also truly indispensable. You're unlikely to *crave*, say, a Gimlet or Negroni, but sometimes only a Bloody will do. Tomato juice and vodka form the core of a Bloody, of course.

Horseradish, celery, olives, and Tabasco often figure in the mix, too. From there, almost anything goes. You have an infinite number of ways to add heat, umami, and character to a Bloody, and that's before you even get to the garnish.

A Bloody has two main components: the base and whatever you spike it with. On the following pages, you'll find our four best Bloody mixes: a pure classic, bold on the horseradish and pepper; a tomatillo variation with heat from Jalapeño and serrano; a juicy base with celery and parsley, so fresh it's almost virtuous; and a Bloody mix with just four ingredients that comes together in moments, so easy it's almost a hack. All four taste mighty nice with vodka or no alcohol at all. Some also pair nicely with mezcal, gin, Bourbon—even Sherry and sake. Mix them up today for a happier tomorrow.

Prepare the Garnish First

Done ahead of time, most of the work for a Bloody Mary goes into making the base. The other potentially time-consuming task? The garnish. Most drinks take just a lemon wheel or maybe a mint sprig, but Bloodies can get a bit more complicated. You're not garnishing with miniature cheeseburgers or a whole fried chicken here, but there's some work involved.

Our tip: Prep your garnish *before* you reach for the booze. You don't want a tray of perspiring Bloodies languishing while you fumble with celery. If the garnish is elaborate— chive-wrapped bacon, ginger-wrapped cucumber—construct those garnishes all at once, laying them on a plate before serving. Even if it's a simpler case of celery stalks and lemon wedges, cut and nicely organize them all first. That's how restaurants can serve approximately 10,000 Bloodies an hour during a busy brunch shift. It's all in the preparation.

Here are our Bloody Mary mixes. Flip to the cocktails starting on page 37 to learn how to spike them or serve them on their own, without alcohol. Just pour over ice and don't skip the garnish.

One note on these mixes: Usually you serve most cocktails as soon as possible, but for Bloodies, it's a different story. These mixes taste better after resting in the fridge overnight. Time allows the many and varied elements—dried spices and grated horseradish chief among them—to steep in the liquid so their flavors integrate and deepen. Make your Bloody mix the day *before* you plan to serve it. The next morning, when you're really ready for that Bloody, most of the work is done already. Just pour, spike, and garnish.

OUR CLASSIC BLOODY MIX

MAKES APPROXIMATELY 32 OUNCES (4 TO 6 DRINKS)

Our version of the classic has quite a few ingredients, but many of them likely are kicking around your fridge and pantry already. You've got umami from the Worcestershire, spice from horseradish and Tabasco, and salinity from the olive brine—everything a Bloody should have.

3 cups tomato juice

6 tablespoons prepared
   horseradish

2 tablespoons
   Worcestershire sauce

1 ounce lemon juice

1 ounce olive brine

6 dashes Tabasco

1 teaspoon celery salt

1 teaspoon coarse ground
   black pepper

1 teaspoon salt

½ teaspoon celery seed

In a quart container, combine all the ingredients and stir thoroughly. Cover and refrigerate overnight. Taste and season with additional salt, pepper, or Tabasco as desired.

TOMATILLO MIX

MAKES 40 OUNCES (6+ DRINKS)

Juicy tomatillos, two different peppers, and the chile-lime of Tajín Clásico Seasoning all come together in this delicious mix. Spike it with mezcal, tequila, or horseradish-infused vodka.

~~~~~~

3 cups tomato juice

6 tomatillos (approximately 450g), quartered

1 tablespoon Worcestershire sauce

1½ teaspoons olive brine

1 ounce lime juice

1 large Jalapeño pepper (approximately 30g), halved lengthwise and seeded

1 serrano pepper segment (approximately 1 inch long, 3g), with seeds

1½ teaspoons Tajín Clásico Seasoning

½ teaspoon salt

In a blender, combine all the ingredients and blend until smooth. Pour into a covered container and refrigerate overnight.

NOTE: If you're unfamiliar with tomatillos, remove their papery husks and stems and wash off the sticky residue before using.

SUPER-CELERY MIX

MAKES 26 OUNCES (4 TO 5 DRINKS)

These days, you'll find riffs on the Bloody Mary with various juices, some swapping out the tomato altogether. But we hold that the tomato is essential, even if you're introducing plenty of other ingredients. Here, you'll build on a tomato base with all kinds of greenery: celery stalks, celery leaves, and parsley. The result has elements of a fresh green juice, without straying too far from a classic Bloody.

2½ cups tomato juice

½ cup loosely packed parsley leaves (approximately 5g)

⅓ cup loosely packed celery leaves (approximately 5g)

1 ounce lemon juice

1 large stalk celery (approximately 75g)

1 piece horseradish (approximately 1 inch long, ½ inch thick, 5g), peeled and diced

½ teaspoon celery salt

½ teaspoon celery seed

In a blender, combine all the ingredients and blend until smooth. Pour into a covered container and refrigerate overnight.

NOTE: Use fresh horseradish root here, rather than the jarred stuff. It can be intense, so treat it as you would a hot pepper. Handle with care, don't touch your face, and, if your eyes water, try to get a little airflow going.

FOUR-INGREDIENT SIMPLE BLOODY MIX

MAKES APPROXIMATELY 32 OUNCES (4 TO 8 DRINKS)

Old Bay Seasoning and clam juice do the heavy lifting for this addictively savory Bloody Mary. Naturally, it has an affinity for a seafood garnish.

3 cups tomato juice

6 ounces bottled clam juice

2 tablespoons Old Bay Seasoning

1 tablespoon prepared horseradish

In a quart container, combine all the ingredients and stir thoroughly. Cover and refrigerate overnight.

BLOODY BEAST

In this remarkable drink, gutsy, bitter Cynar balances smooth, boozy bourbon. It's a profoundly complex cocktail that stands up to all the powerful flavors in a Bloody Mary as well as the intensity of bacon (optional . . . kind of).

〜〜〜〜〜〜〜〜〜〜〜〜〜〜〜〜〜〜〜〜〜〜〜〜〜〜〜〜〜〜〜〜

4 ounces Our Classic Bloody
 Mix (page 34)

1 ounce Bourbon

½ ounce Cynar

1 lemon wheel for garnish

1 strip bacon, 4 inches long,
 for garnish

In a large rocks glass over ice, combine all the ingredients. Stir briefly. Garnish with a lemon wheel and, even better, bacon.

TIP: For visual impact, halve a 4-inch strip of bacon lengthwise, stack the halves, and tie three chives in a knot around the middle.

SUNRISE MARY

A Bloody Mary doesn't need a lot of hard alcohol—or any at all—to taste delicious. Here, our fresh Super-Celery Mix gets a boost from dry, nuanced fino Sherry, which introduces a ton of complexity without a lot of booze. If you're serving this for brunch, you can't go wrong with a jamón-wrapped olive for garnish.

〜〜〜〜〜〜〜〜〜〜〜〜〜〜〜〜〜〜〜〜〜〜〜〜〜〜〜〜〜〜〜〜

1½ ounces fino Sherry

6 ounces Super-Celery Mix
 (page 36)

1 lemon wheel for garnish

1 green olive for garnish

Jamón serrano or prosciutto
 for garnish

In a Collins glass filled with ice, combine the Sherry and celery mix, and stir briefly. Garnish with a lemon wheel and, since we love a meaty garnish, a green olive on a skewer wrapped in *jamón serrano* (ideally) or prosciutto.

Our Best Bloody
(drink + carafe)

Green Snapper

OUR BEST BLOODY

This one's for the traditionalists. Vodka is our pick, but feel free to swap in tequila, white rum, or any spirit you like.

1½ ounces vodka

6 ounces Our Classic Bloody
   Mix (page 34)

1 stalk celery for garnish

1 lemon wedge for garnish

1 green olive for garnish

Tabasco (optional)

In a Collins glass filled with ice, add the vodka and bloody mix, and stir briefly. Garnish with a celery stick, lemon wedge, and an olive. If you like it spicy, add some Tabasco for extra heat.

GREEN SNAPPER

A Red Snapper describes a Bloody Mary with gin swapped for vodka. Our Super-Celery Mix pairs brilliantly with the herbaceous spirit, and our gin of choice for this recipe is The Botanist. The garnish is all kinds of green.

1½ ounces gin

6 ounces Super-Celery Mix
   (page 36)

1 stalk celery, leaves on, for
   garnish

1 lemon wedge for garnish

3 or 4 sprigs parsley for
   garnish

In a Collins glass filled with ice, combine gin and celery mix, and stir briefly. Garnish with the stalk of celery (with the leaves), lemon wedge, and parsley sprigs.

MEZCAL MARIA

Our spicy Tomatillo Mix makes a great match for smoky mezcal. Go all out with a Tajín Clásico Seasoning rim and pickled tomatillos to garnish, because the best Bloodies always come with a snack.

Tajín Clásico Seasoning for
  rim (optional)
1½ ounces mezcal
6 ounces Tomatillo Mix
  (page 35)
Pickled tomatillo and onion
  for garnish
1 lime wheel for garnish

If desired, rim a Collins glass with Tajín Clásico Seasoning. In the prepared glass filled with ice, combine the mezcal and tomatillo mix, and stir briefly. Garnish with a pickled tomatillo and onion and a thin lime wheel.

HAIL MARY

If you really love the sharp bite of horseradish, here's how to dial it up. Infusing vodka with horseradish root gives you the most concentrated, spicy, sinus-tingling power. You'll love it with the balanced heat of the Tomatillo Mix.

1½ ounces Horseradish-
  Infused Vodka (page 261)
6 ounces Tomatillo Mix
  (page 35)
1 stalk celery for garnish
1 lime wedge for garnish
1 pickled Jalapeño pepper
  for garnish (optional)

In a Collins glass filled with ice, combine the vodka and tomatillo mix, and stir briefly. Garnish with a celery stalk, a lime wedge, and, if you like, a pickled Jalapeño pepper.

CHESAPEAKE BLOODY

Some Bloody Marys have more than a dozen ingredients, and they're all the better for it. Not this guy. Our Four-Ingredient Simple Bloody Mix perfectly suits a big pour of vodka, letting the varied flavors of Old Bay and briny clam juice from the mix shine through loud and clear. Not every Bloody deserves a shrimp, but this one does.

1½ ounces vodka

6 ounces Four-Ingredient
 Simple Bloody Mix
 (page 36)

1 lemon wedge for garnish

1 cocktail shrimp, chilled,
 for garnish (optional)

In a Collins glass filled with ice, combine the vodka and Four-Ingredient Simple Bloody Mix and stir briefly. Garnish with the lemon wedge and, if it's brunchtime, a chilled cocktail shrimp.

SAKE MARY

Here's another Bloody big on flavor but lower on alcohol. Sake echoes the umami and salinity of our clam-spiked Old Bay Mix. Don't skip the sushi bar–inspired garnish.

3 ounces sake

4 ounces Four-Ingredient
 Simple Bloody Mix
 (page 36)

3 cucumber spears for
 garnish

1 thin slice of pickled ginger
 for garnish

In a Collins glass filled with ice, combine the sake and the Four-Ingredient Simple Bloody Mix and stir briefly. Garnish with 3 thin cucumber spears wrapped in pickled ginger and skewered.

3.

COBBLERS

JUICY · CHILLY · DELIGHTFUL

Let's make a Cobbler . . .

Far less widely known than many other drinks today, the Cobbler was a 19th-century favorite in America that popularized two now-indispensable elements of drinking culture: ice and the straw. How many cocktails can claim that?

The essence of a Cobbler is crushed ice or the pebbly shaped "cobbled" ice that likely gave the drink its name. Above all, a Cobbler is a refreshing, cooling drink created in a world without air-conditioning or electric fans. Some boozy Cobblers existed back then, but Sherry and other wine-based Cobblers proved much more popular. You can drink this refreshing and low-proof cocktail all day. But it's difficult to sip from the bottom of the drink with all that ice. Ergo the straw.

Some drinks don't take well to a ton of fruit flavors thrown at them. Some, on the other hand, take *really* well to that. There's not much we find tastier than citrus and Sherry put together atop tons of ice. The result is a Cobbler, as low-proof and easygoing as a Mint Julep is boozy and traditional. These recipes might stray a bit from the classic, but it's all in service of delicious drinking. If smashing up fruit and Sherry is wrong, we don't want to be right.

BUY THESE BOTTLES

Sherries vary widely, so it's essential to purchase the correct style. A fino and an oloroso differ as much as (if not more than) a Pinot Grigio and a Cabernet Sauvignon. You can find many excellent brands. Sold nationally, González Byass and Lustau are two great choices. Look for González Byass fino Sherry by its proper name: Tio Pepe.

DON'T SKIP THE STRAW

You want a short straw for a Cobbler, a few inches above the rim of your glass. If you don't have a metal julep straw, consider a paper straw that you can cut to your preferred length. Yes, paper straws can become mushy quickly, but fear not. These Cobblers taste so good that they won't last long.

OUR SHERRY COBBLER

The Sherry Cobblers of yore most often used orange as the starring fruit, which is why we use it in our slightly-more-out-there recipes. But the alchemy of Sherry and orange is something so special, it's a drink all in itself. The depth of flavor from so few ingredients will amaze you.

¼ navel orange, cut into
    two pieces
    (approximately 80g)
2½ ounces Amontillado
    Sherry
½ ounce Simple Syrup
    (page 255)
3 orange slices for garnish
Berries of choice for garnish

In the bottom of a cocktail shaker, muddle the orange pieces thoroughly. Add the remaining ingredients and ice and shake vigorously. Double strain into a wine glass or large bowl-shaped glass filled with ice (ideally crushed ice or pellet ice). Garnish with thin, half-moon slices of orange and lots of berries. Serve with a straw.

IN LIVING COLOR

Light, dry manzanilla Sherry meets raspberry and orange in this bright, summery, slurpable sunburst of a cocktail. It's the perfect drink to go big with the garnish.

1 large orange wedge
    (⅛ navel orange, approxi-
    mately 40g), halved
½ lemon with peel
    (approximately 30g),
    quartered
15 raspberries
    (approximately 50g)
3 ounces manzanilla Sherry
1 ounce Honey Syrup
    (page 255)
3 orange slices for garnish
3 lemon wheels for garnish
5 raspberries for garnish

In the bottom of a cocktail shaker, muddle the orange and lemon pieces thoroughly. Add the raspberries and muddle again but more gently. Add the remaining ingredients and ice and shake vigorously. Double-strain into a wine glass or large bowl-shaped glass filled with ice, ideally crushed or pellet. Garnish away with 3 thin half-moon slices of orange, 3 thin lemon wheels, and raspberries. Serve with a paper straw or two.

NOTE: Don't substitute a standard lemon for a Meyer. Meyer lemons taste considerably sweeter, and their flavor defines this cocktail.

In Praise of Sherry

We get so excited about Sherry, and we hope that, after trying it in cocktails, you will, too. It has something of a bad reputation as sweet and a little fusty. (It doesn't help that cooking Sherry, sold at most grocery stores, tastes awful on its own.) But Sherry has an astonishing diversity of flavor. A Spanish fortified wine—meaning wine with distilled alcohol added—its styles differ in the extent of their aging and exposure to oxygen.

Sherry has an entire world of history and taxonomy to explore, but for cocktails? These deeply complex wines can add a savory, nutty, or vinous element to drinks without contributing too much alcohol. Whether using them to mellow a Hot Toddy, enliven a Martini, or, here, as the basis for vibrant Cobblers, they're a bartender's secret weapon—and delicious sipped straight, too.

Styles You Should Know

FINO ("FINE"): As light-bodied and dry as the driest white wine but a bit higher in alcohol, around 15% ABV. Look for Tio Pepe, a widely available brand. Use it in light-bodied cocktails or sip it ice-cold from a wine glass on a sweaty summer evening.

MANZANILLA ("CHAMOMILE"): Similar to fino, often with light salinity. The name describes the color and the aroma.

AMONTILLADO ("FROM MONTILLA"): With some oxidative aging, it develops a complex, nutty character and a light brown hue; sensational in Cobblers, around 17.5% ABV.

OLOROSO ("SCENTED"): With far more time in the barrel than other styles, oloroso Sherries develop a rich brown color and notes of dried fruit. Generally around 20% ABV, these add an elusive, hard-to-pinpoint depth to cocktails, particularly with dark spirits.

PEDRO XIMÉNEZ (NAME OF THE GRAPE VARIETY): Sometimes abbreviated to "PX," these Sherries taste sweet and deeply concentrated, all raisin and spice, with a more viscous texture. Use as a sweetener in cocktails, such as an Old-Fashioned, or sip slowly after dinner.

STRAWBERRY RHUBARB COBBLER

What, a dessert? No, not that kind of strawberry rhubarb cobbler. Here, fresh rhubarb, not cooked down with sugar, delivers zingy acidity that slices through the berry sweetness. With Amontillado Sherry, it tastes even better.

Using rhubarb here doesn't require a long steep or a juicer. Our quick and easy strawberry rhubarb blender syrup comes together in about one minute. Just whiz the ingredients with simple syrup, strain, and you're ready to go. Almost as fast as muddling.

1 large orange wedge (⅛ navel orange, approximately 40g), halved

2½ ounces Amontillado Sherry

2½ ounces Strawberry Rhubarb Blender Syrup (page 258)

3 orange slices for garnish

2 rhubarb slices for garnish

½ small strawberry for garnish

In the bottom of a cocktail shaker, muddle the orange pieces thoroughly. Add the remaining ingredients and ice and shake vigorously. Double strain into a wine glass or large bowl-shaped glass filled with ice, ideally crushed or pellet. Garnish with 3 three half-moon slices of orange, 2 thin slices of rhubarb, and half a strawberry. Serve with a paper straw or two.

HELLO SUNSHINE

If you've ever had a fresh Meyer lemon, you know how remarkably vibrant it can taste. Dry fino Sherry offers the perfect counterpoint, not taking center stage but highlighting the citrus's bold flavor.

1 small Meyer lemon (approximately 50g), quartered

½ orange slice (¼ inch thick, approximately 10g)

2½ ounces fino Sherry

½ ounce Simple Syrup (page 255)

1 orange slice for garnish

1 small Meyer lemon wedge for garnish

5 blueberries for garnish

1 sprig mint for garnish

In the bottom of a cocktail shaker, muddle the lemon and orange pieces thoroughly. Add the remaining ingredients and ice and shake vigorously. Double strain into a wine glass or large bowl-shaped glass filled with ice, ideally crushed or pellet. Garnish with a half-moon slice of orange, Meyer lemon wedge, blueberries, and sprig of mint. Serve with a paper straw or two.

NOTE: Don't substitute a standard lemon for a Meyer. Meyer lemons taste considerably sweeter, and their flavor defines this cocktail.

TRICK MIRROR

How can a drink simultaneously be so refreshing and so mysterious? Elusive notes of Sherry, rum, and gentian swirling in a bright backdrop of citrus make this a truly memorable cocktail. Use a dark, brooding rum, such as Diplomático, here.

¼ navel orange (approximately 80g), halved

1½ ounces oloroso Sherry

1 ounce dark rum

½ ounce Lo-Fi Gentian Amaro (page 27)

½ ounce Raw Sugar Syrup (page 256)

3 orange slices for garnish

3 blackberries for garnish

In the bottom of a cocktail shaker, muddle the orange pieces thoroughly. Add the remaining ingredients and ice and shake vigorously. Double strain into a wine glass or large bowl-shaped glass filled with ice, ideally crushed or pellet. Garnish with 3 thin half-moon slices of orange and 3 blackberries. Serve with a paper straw or two.

TRANSATLANTIC

A Cobbler Margarita? Dry Sherry and Tequila blanco ("clear") make one of our favorite pairings. A good low-proof Tequila drink highlights the spirit's flavors while keeping the booze in check.

~~~~~~

¼ ruby red grapefruit (approximately 100g), halved

1 lime wedge (approximately 15g)

½ orange slice (¼ inch thick, approximately 10g)

1½ ounces fino Sherry

1 ounce Tequila blanco

1 ounce Light Agave Syrup (page 255)

1 orange slice for garnish

1 grapefruit slice for garnish

1 lime wedge for garnish

In the bottom of a cocktail shaker, muddle the grapefruit, lime, and orange pieces thoroughly. Add the remaining ingredients and ice and shake vigorously. Double strain into a wine glass or large bowl-shaped glass filled with ice, ideally crushed or pellet. Garnish with a thin half-moon slice of orange, a thin half-moon slice of grapefruit, and lime wedge. Serve with a paper straw or two.

4.

DAIQUIRÍS

TART · CRISP · VERSATILE

I'd like a Daiquirí . . .

This true classic so often is misunderstood. Just like the Mai Tai, its rum cousin, a Daiquirí in the popular imagination—tall, frosty, and served at a tropical resort—runs a far cry from its original form. A real and true Daiquirí has four ingredients: white rum, lime, sugar, and ice. That's it, no slushie machines, no artificially flavored fruit syrups, no umbrellas. A properly made Daiquirí tastes bright with fresh lime juice, refreshing as anything, and dangerous in its drinkability. (Even thirst-quenching cocktails can pack a punch.) A member of the sour family—spirit, citrus, sweetener, shaken—it shares cocktail DNA with the Whiskey Sour, Gimlet, and Margarita.

As with so many cocktails, it's impossible to account for the definitive history of the Daiquirí because it turns out that drinkers aren't always the most disciplined documentarians. (Imagine that.) Refining sugar creates molasses, and distilling molasses creates rum. Figuring out who first combined them with a little lime would be futile, to say the least. As cocktail historian Dave Wondrich once memorably wrote: "The Daiquirí represents such an obvious marriage between local ingredients—rum, sugar, limes—that it would take the chowder-headedest duffer who ever buttoned a trouser not to invent it."

The version we know today, appearing in cocktail books and manuals for more than a century, traces its lineage to 19th-century Cuba. During the Spanish-American War, which began in 1898, an American mining engineer named Jennings Cox Jr. was working near Daiquirí, a small town on Cuba's southern coast. The story goes that, while entertaining guests, Cox found himself short on gin, his tipple of choice, and reached for local white rum instead. He added lime and sugar, ingredients on hand, and created the Daiquirí. By 1909, a sailor who had passed through Cuba introduced the drink to the Army and Navy Club of Washington, DC, and the drink's popularity grew from there. Cuba also gave rise to the frozen Daiquirí, first devised in the 1930s at el Floridita, one of Ernest Hemingway's legendary Havana haunts, back when blenders were the novel technology of the day. So we can credit

Havana for the frozen Daiquirí, too—notwithstanding the slushy drinks from premade mixes that snowballed at the end of the 20th century.

In Cuba and America alike, the Daiquirí endures because of its simplicity. Contemporary bartenders embrace it wholeheartedly. Delightful in its own right, it also offers a great template for riffing. Many fruity and herbal flavors pair beautifully with lime and rum. Swapping out white rum for rich and funky Jamaican rum yields a totally different effect. Go the other direction and lighten it with wine-based Lillet. Campari can add a pleasantly bitter element, and hibiscus a fresh and fragrant one. We still can't get behind syrupy-sweet slushies, but a well-made frozen Daiquirí tastes truly delicious.

BUY THESE BOTTLES

A staggeringly diverse category, rum runs from clean white liquors to brooding, complex sippers. For most Daiquirís, you want white rum. Some white spirits (vodka or gin) don't age, but white rums typically age in barrels and then go through filtration to strip the color. As a result, even white rums often have good body and substance, whereas vodka generally feels thinner on the palate.

Our favorite for Daiquirís: Banks 5 Island Blend Rum. A blend of more than 20 rums from across the Caribbean, it tastes dry and clean but with real character, a phenomenal base for classic drinks. Other great rums include Brugal Extra Dry from the Dominican Republic and Flor de Caña 4 Year Extra Seco from Nicaragua. Why not Cuban rum, for a Cuban cocktail? Well, in America, you can't buy it. (The Saga of Cuban Rum on page 63 tells the tale.)

OUR CLASSIC DAIQUIRÍ

Rum, lime, sugar—three bar staples that taste better together. Bartenders differ in their preferred ratios for a Daiquirí, but this spec gives you a tart and boozy drink with just enough sugar for good balance.

2 ounces white rum

1 ounce lime juice

¾ ounce Simple Syrup
(page 255)

1 lime wheel for garnish

In a cocktail shaker, combine all the ingredients. Fill the shaker with ice and seal it. Shake vigorously for 15 seconds and double strain into a chilled coupe. Garnish by floating a thin lime wheel on top.

UP OR ROCKS?

Some drinks always are served "up," generally in a coupe, without ice. A Martini is the classic example. Others generally are served "on the rocks," meaning over ice in a rocks glass. You'll always see an Old-Fashioned served this way. A Daiquirí can go either way. We love the elegance of a classic Daiquirí in a coupe. On the other hand, a drink on the rocks can handle a more elaborate garnish, and the ice keeps the drink cooler for longer. If you'd prefer any of these drinks on the rocks, rather than up—or vice versa—switch away. If you do serve them up in a coupe, always chill the glass first (page 16) and double strain the drink to remove any ice chips. Life's too short for a warm Daiquirí.

DAIQUIRÍ IN THE AFTERNOON

It may not taste strong, and it may go down easily, but with 2 full ounces of rum, a classic Daiquirí is a powerful cocktail. Let's lighten in up. Here, you're keeping the Daiquirí's tart, snappy character but dialing down the alcohol just a bit. Wine-based Lillet and coconut water seamlessly integrate with light rum for a drink that tastes no less delicious, despite its lower ABV.

1½ ounces white rum

1 ounce coconut water

½ ounce Lillet

½ ounce lime juice

½ ounce Simple Syrup
(page 255)

3 lime wheels for garnish

In a cocktail shaker, combine all the ingredients. Fill the shaker with ice and seal it. Shake vigorously for 15 seconds and strain into a rocks glass filled with ice. Garnish with 3 thin lime wheels.

BATCH IT

For 6 drinks, you'll need 9 ounces white rum, 3 ounces Lillet, 6 ounces coconut water, 3 ounces lime juice, 3 ounces simple syrup, 6 ounces water to replicate the ice melt from shaking, and 6 lime wheels for garnish. In a pitcher, stir it all with ice to chill everything down. Pour 5 ounces over more ice per glass. Garnish with the lime wheels, and you're ready for a summer party.

RASPBERRY DAIQUIRÍ

*Like corn on the cob or vine-ripened tomatoes, a fresh raspberry is one of those pure
tastes of summer. Once you've made a quick raspberry syrup, just shake it with rum
and lime for a summery Daiquirí that has a flavor as vivid as its bright pink hue.*

2 ounces white rum

1 ounce lime juice

¾ ounce Raspberry Syrup
(page 257)

1 lemon peel for garnish

1 raspberry for garnish

In a cocktail shaker, combine all the ingredients. Fill the
shaker with ice and seal it. Shake vigorously for 15 seconds and double strain into a chilled coupe. Express the
strip of lemon peel, 2 to 3 inches long, skin side down,
over the surface of the drink. Run the skin side of the
peel around the rim of the glass to distribute the citrus
oils, then add the peel, skin side up, to the cocktail. Garnish with the raspberry on a cocktail pick.

BATCH IT

Achieving raspberry flavor through a homemade syrup—no messy muddling—makes this
drink easy to batch for events. One 6-ounce
container of raspberries yields enough syrup for
about 12 drinks.

For 6 drinks, combine 1½ cups white rum, 6 ounces lime juice,
4½ ounces raspberry syrup, and 6 ounces water in a quart container with a watertight lid. Refrigerate until ready to serve.

To serve, shake the container hard to combine the ingredients.
Divide equally among six chilled coupes, just under 5 ounces per
glass, and garnish each with a raspberry and a lemon peel strip.
Alternately, you can pour it all into a pitcher with ice and let guests
serve themselves; just make sure no one pours too heavy!

For 12 drinks, double this recipe in two separate containers.

SCARLET DAIQUIRÍ

The adaptable Daiquirí takes well to Campari's bitter bite, which, here, you'll balance with fresh strawberry. If you like drinks with fruit—but not overly sweet "fruity" drinks—this one's for you. Don't skip the garnish; the fresh scent of the orange pulls the whole drink together.

3 strawberries (approximately 50g), hulled and quartered

1½ ounces white rum

½ ounce Campari

¾ ounce lime juice

¾ ounce Simple Syrup (page 255)

1 dash orange bitters

1 orange wheel for garnish

1 strawberry for garnish

In the bottom of a cocktail shaker, firmly muddle the strawberry pieces until broken and releasing their juice. Add the remaining ingredients and ice and shake vigorously for 15 seconds. Double strain into a rocks glass filled with ice. Garnish with an orange wheel curved around the interior rim of the glass and a strawberry.

FROZEN DAIQUIRÍS

MAKES 2 DRINKS

No introduction needed. Get the proportions of rum, lime juice, sugar, and ice correct, and it's easy to whiz up a blender of slushies that taste just right.

- **3 ounces white rum**
- **2 ounces lime juice**
- **2 ounces Simple Syrup (page 255)**
- **2 lime wheels for garnish**

In a blender, combine all the ingredients and add 2 cups of ice. Blend until smooth and divide between chilled rocks or Collins glasses. Garnish with 2 thin lime wheels.

NOTE: You may have spotted that this Daiquirí, like all our frozen drinks, contains a higher proportion of simple syrup. Why? Cold suppresses the perception of sweetness, so you need a bit more sweetener for a comparable-tasting drink.

For 6 drinks or 4 big ones, follow the directions above, just increase the amounts. Go with 9 ounces white rum, 6 ounces lime juice, 6 ounces simple syrup, and 6 cups of ice.

PAPA COCO

Ernest Hemingway was a notorious drinker. Created in his honor, the Hemingway Daiquirí (also called the Papa Doble) has twice the usual measure of rum. Suffice it to say, the drinks he allegedly favored weren't necessarily known for their quality but for their strength.

The Hemingway Daiquirí, made with grapefruit and maraschino liqueur, serves as the inspiration for this frozen drink. But rather than drowning it in extra rum, you'll use coconut water to lighten it, leaving it refreshing rather than aggressive.

3 ounces white rum

2 ounces coconut water

1½ ounces Simple Syrup (page 255)

1 ounce ruby red grapefruit juice

½ ounce lime juice

¼ ounce maraschino liqueur

In a blender, combine all the ingredients and add 2 cups of ice. Blend until smooth and divide between chilled rocks or Collins glasses. No garnish necessary; serve with a straw if you like.

BATCH IT

For 6 drinks, follow the directions above, just increase the amounts. Go with 9 ounces white rum, 6 ounces coconut water, 3 ounces ruby red grapefruit juice, 1½ ounces lime juice, ¾ ounce maraschino liqueur, 4½ ounces simple syrup, and 6 cups of ice.

HAVANA BLUES

MAKES 2 DRINKS

A good frozen Daiquirí = fun. A blue *frozen Daiquirí =* way more fun. *Most blue drinks get their color from blue Curaçao, an orange liqueur with food coloring that tastes sticky and muted. Split the blue stuff with the king of orange liqueurs, rich and tasty Grand Marnier, for the ultimate highbrow-lowbrow move.*

3 ounces white rum

1½ ounces lime juice

1½ ounces Simple Syrup
   (page 255)

1 ounce Grand Marnier

½ ounce blue Curaçao

10 dashes orange bitters

1 orange slice for garnish

2 pineapple wedges, rind on,
   for garnish

1 strawberry, halved, for
   garnish

In a blender, combine all the ingredients and add 2 cups of ice. Blend until smooth and divide between chilled rocks or Collins glasses. Garnish each drink with a half-moon slice of orange, pineapple wedge, and half a strawberry.

BATCH IT

It's easy to blend a whole round at once, and it's *bright blue.* What could work better for a summer party?

For 6 drinks, follow the directions above, just increase the amounts. Go with 9 ounces white rum, 3 ounces Grand Marnier, 1½ ounces blue Curaçao, 4½ ounces lime juice, 4½ ounces simple syrup, 30 dashes of bitters, and 6 cups of ice. Garnish as directed.

BANANA BOAT

You've heard of orange liqueur; maybe you've heard of berry liqueurs, such as Chambord or Cassis. But banana liqueur? It may sound improbable, but Banane du Bresil from French producer Giffard tastes out of this world. As fruits go, bananas are among the most difficult to work into cocktails. They don't really juice, they have a unique texture, and their mellow flavor often gets lost. But Banane du Bresil captures the fruit's distinctive taste in a bottle. One of our favorite uses for it? A dark Daiquirí with a compelling tropical vibe.

2 ounces dark rum

¾ ounce Giffard Banane du Bresil

¾ ounce lime juice

½ ounce Simple Syrup (page 255)

1 dash Angostura bitters

1 lime peel for garnish

In a cocktail shaker, combine all the ingredients. Fill the shaker with ice and seal it. Shake vigorously for 15 seconds and strain into a rocks glass filled with ice. Express a 2-inch strip of lime peel, skin side down, over the surface of the drink, run the skin around the rim of the glass to distribute the citrus oils, and add the peel, skin side up, to the cocktail.

TIP: For a fun additional garnish, skewer two diagonally cut frozen slices of banana on a cocktail pick.

BUY THIS BOTTLE

Giffard Banane du Bresil

MALAGUEÑA II

Light rum makes for crisp and clean Daiquirís. Darker rum makes them richer and weightier, the better to sip slowly and savor. Here's the perfect Daiquirí for fall, combining complex, funky Jamaican rum and friendly, fragrant allspice. We recommend Appleton Estate Reserve rum for this one.

2 ounces Jamaican rum

1 ounce lime juice

¾ ounce Raw Sugar Syrup (page 256)

¼ ounce allspice dram

1 dash Angostura bitters

1 lime wheel for garnish

In a cocktail shaker, combine all the ingredients. Fill the shaker with ice and seal it. Shake vigorously for 15 seconds and strain into a rocks glass filled with ice. Garnish with a thin lime wheel.

BELOW DECK

Popular in many parts of the world—including West Africa, the Caribbean, and Latin America—hibiscus (also called sorrel) has an unmistakable tart and vibrant flavor that we love in cocktails. Here, it contributes its vivid purple hue and powerful character for an added herbal dimension. You can make our hibiscus syrup in a flash: You need just hibiscus teabags, sugar, and hot water.

1½ ounces white rum

¾ ounce lime juice

¾ ounce Hibiscus Syrup (page 258)

10 leaves mint (approximately 3g)

1 dash orange bitters

3 sprigs mint for garnish

In a cocktail shaker, combine all the ingredients. Fill the shaker with ice and seal it. Shake vigorously for 15 seconds and double strain into a rocks glass filled with ice. Tap the sprigs of mint lightly against your hand to release their fragrant oils before garnishing the glass with them.

EVERY COCKTAIL HAS A TWIST

The Saga of Cuban Rum

It makes perfect sense to make the Daiquirí, a Cuban drink, with Cuban rum, but you can't buy Cuban rum in 21st-century America. For that, you can thank the Kennedy administration and every Congress and administration thereafter.

During the early 1900s—particularly during the 13 unlucky years of Prohibition, when America's legal bars shut down, pushing cocktail culture to the Caribbean—Cuba became a popular destination for American travelers. Robust trade existed between the two countries, and Havana in particular played a role in pop culture similarly as Las Vegas does today. But following the 1959 Cuban Revolution and Fidel Castro's rise to power, America cut diplomatic ties with Cuba and, in 1962, imposed a near-total trade embargo that largely persists to this day.

After the revolution, the Cuban government nationalized Havana Club, a leading Cuban rum producer. After decades of sales limited to the domestic market and Communist Eastern Europe, the company formed a partnership with liquor giant Pernod Ricard in 1993, enabling global distribution—global with the exception of America, that is. Over the next decade, Havana Club became one of the world's leading rum brands, with widespread international success.

Meanwhile, the Bacardí family—you may have heard of their rum—who had fled Cuba for Puerto Rico during the revolution, purchased the lapsed Havana Club trademark in America. They sell a rum of their own, not produced in Cuba, under the "Havana Club" name, which triggered a copyright lawsuit still mired in the American courts.

So the Havana Club made by Bacardi and sold in America isn't Cuban rum, but the Havana Club sold in Cuba and the rest of the world, but not America, is. (Got that?) It's illegal to sell Cuban-made products in the States or import them for commercial purposes, but, thanks to a 2015 liberalization in American policy, it's perfectly legal to bring a few bottles of Cuban rum into the States for personal consumption. You don't need to go to Cuba for it, either. If only Cuban Havana Club will do, grab a bottle at a duty-free shop the next time you pass through Asia or Europe. Rum tastes better well traveled.

5.

EGGNOGS

MERRY · RICH · NOSTALGIC

DOWN TO BASES

Let's make our Eggnog . . .

A winter staple and indispensable at holiday gatherings, Eggnog serves as a yearly tradition for many. It's easy enough to buy some at the store, but once you make your own and realize how simple the process can be, you won't go back. Thanks to various stabilizers, store-bought Eggnogs can drink thick and gloppy, settling heavily in your stomach. Homemade Eggnog tastes lighter, more drinkable, and just, well, *better.*

So how do you make Eggnog? You've got a few options. If you really want to impress your guests—and you're going to make it right before you serve it—you separate fresh eggs. You then whip the egg whites in a food processor until they form soft, frothy peaks and fold them into the richer, yolky base. The result is a sophisticated Eggnog with an uncommonly light texture. But if you want to make it in advance—or just get the 'Nog in a glass as fast as possible—pull out the blender.

Pour in milk, sugar, cream, whole eggs, and nutmeg and whiz it all together. Who doesn't love a good holiday shortcut?

Once made, your Eggnog tastes delicious as is, no alcohol required. But this is a cocktail book, so you probably are looking for a little more. We're adding classic spirits, such as Bourbon and rum; less common spirits, including Scotch; and for something lighter and less orthodox: vodka. Even a good liqueur can find a home in Eggnog.

DOWN TO BASES ·································○

If you're looking for the platonic ideal of Eggnog—rich in flavor, silky in texture—you'll want to separate the yolks and whites and then whip each separately. If you drink the Eggnog right away, you'll be amazed how light such a creamy drink can taste. For a time-saving shortcut, just dump whole eggs in a blender with all the other ingredients and blend until frothy. Use either method to create a 'Nog base you can drink on its own or spike with some (holiday) spirits.

SILKIEST BASE

MAKES APPROXIMATELY 20 OUNCES (4 TO 6 DRINKS)

4 large eggs, separated

3 tablespoons granulated white sugar, divided

1 cup whole milk

½ cup heavy cream

¼ teaspoon ground nutmeg

To the food processor, add the egg whites and 1 tablespoon of the sugar. Pulse until soft peaks form. Transfer to a clean bowl and set aside. Wash the processor bowl.

Add the yolks to the processor bowl and blend until runny and smooth. Add the milk, cream, remaining 2 tablespoons of sugar, and nutmeg. Blend until ingredients incorporate fully and the sugar dissolves completely. Gently fold the yolk mixture into the whites. Cover the bowl or pour into a container with a lid and refrigerate until ready to use. We recommend serving it or making cocktails with it as soon as possible, once chilled, to preserve that light, silky texture.

BLENDER BASE

MAKES APPROXIMATELY 20 OUNCES (4 TO 6 DRINKS)

4 large eggs

3 tablespoons granulated white sugar

1 cup whole milk

½ cup heavy cream

¼ teaspoon ground nutmeg

In a blender, add the eggs and then the rest of the ingredients. Blend until they incorporate fully. Transfer to a sealable container or a bottle with a lid and chill thoroughly before serving.

OLD-FASHIONED EGGNOG

You'll taste the Bourbon in this Eggnog, but it won't take over.

〜〜〜〜〜〜〜〜〜〜〜〜〜〜〜〜〜〜

**3 ounces chilled Eggnog
base of choice (page 66)**
1½ ounces Bourbon
**Freshly grated nutmeg for
garnish**

In a rocks glass, combine the ingredients and stir gently. Garnish with the grated nutmeg.

MORE WAYS TO SPIKE YOUR 'NOG

Classic additions to Eggnog include dark rum, Bourbon, and brandy, but feel free to experiment. For a lightly alcoholic, flavorful version, add 1 ounce of spirit to 3 ounces of base. For a boozier sipper, add up to 2 ounces of spirit.

For bigger batches, stay on the lighter side. Start with 6 ounces of spirit per 18 to 20 ounces of base. It's easier to add just a little more spirit to taste than to run out of base.

RUN RUN RUDOLPH

This creamy Eggnog has the classic flavors of an Irish coffee. We recommend Tullamore D.E.W. as the whiskey and the excellent cold brew liqueur Mr. Black. Santa definitely would appreciate one.

3 ounces chilled Eggnog
 base of choice (page 66)
1 ounce Irish whiskey
½ ounce coffee liqueur
Freshly grated nutmeg for
 garnish

In a rocks glass, combine the ingredients and stir gently. Garnish with the grated nutmeg.

For 6 drinks, combine 18 to 20 ounces of chilled base, 6 ounces Irish whiskey, and 3 ounces coffee liqueur. Pour into rocks glasses and garnish with freshly grated nutmeg.

EGGNOG FOSTER

A holiday drink crossed with bananas Foster, this Eggnog drinks like dessert all by itself. The oloroso Sherry takes it into fancy-cocktail territory.

3 ounces chilled Eggnog
 base of choice (page 66)
1 ounce dark rum
1 ounce Giffard Banane du
 Bresil (page 61)
½ ounce oloroso Sherry
 (optional)
Freshly grated nutmeg for
 garnish

In a rocks glass, combine the ingredients and stir gently. Garnish with the grated nutmeg.

For 6 drinks, combine 18 to 20 ounces chilled Eggnog base, 6 ounces dark rum, and 6 ounces banana liqueur, plus 3 ounces oloroso Sherry, if using. Pour into rocks glasses and garnish with freshly grated nutmeg.

Run Run Rudolph

'NOGMANAY

This offbeat Eggnog makes use of an intense, slightly wild single malt Scotch, Laphroaig 10 Year, and the powerfully flavored The King's Ginger liqueur for a robust holiday drink.

4 ounces chilled Eggnog
  base of choice (page 66)
¾ ounce The King's Ginger
½ ounce Laphroaig 10 Year
1 dash Fee Brothers Old
  Fashioned Aromatic
  Bitters
Freshly grated nutmeg for
  garnish
1 dehydrated orange wheel
  for garnish (optional)

In a rocks glass, combine the ingredients and stir gently. Garnish with the grated nutmeg and, should you have one in your cocktail arsenal, a dehydrated orange wheel.

BATCH IT

For 6 drinks, combine 18 to 20 ounces chilled Eggnog base, 4½ ounces The King's Ginger, 3 ounces Laphroaig 10 Year, and 6 dashes Fee Brothers Old Fashioned Aromatic Bitters. Pour into rocks glasses and garnish with freshly grated nutmeg and dehydrated orange wheels, if desired.

DON'T FORGET THE NUTMEG

Some garnishes are optional. Nutmeg on Eggnog is absolutely not. Omitting it would be like omitting pumpkin spice from a pumpkin pie. The nutmeg flavor specifically helps us recognize a drink as Eggnog rather than any old creamy drink.

Also, ground nutmeg will suffice, but grating it fresh amps up the aromatics. You can buy a jar of whole nutmeg pods at any grocery store, and it'll last you through the season. Use a fine microplane to grate it.

SINGLE-SERVING EGGNOG

Maybe you're not making Eggnog for the whole family; maybe you just need a 'Nog for yourself. If so, don't break out the blender. You can make a single-serve version right in your cocktail shaker. The key to any egg drink is the "double shake." First, combine all the ingredients in a cocktail shaker without ice and shake hard, which breaks up the egg and emulsifies it with the other ingredients. Then open your shaker, add ice, and shake again to chill it down.

1 large egg

2 ounces Bourbon, dark rum, brandy, or a combination

1 ounce half-and-half

1 ounce Simple Syrup (page 255)

Freshly grated nutmeg for garnish

In a cocktail shaker, add the egg and then the rest of the ingredients. Shake hard for 15 seconds. Open the shaker, add ice, and shake again for 15 seconds. Strain into a rocks glass and garnish with the grated nutmeg.

WORKING WITH RAW EGGS

Raw eggs can seem like an intimidating ingredient, but working with them doesn't have to be difficult. A little common sense goes a long way. Use fresher eggs, not from a carton nearing its expiration date. Also give the cracked eggs a look and a sniff before using. Tip: Add the egg to your shaker as the first ingredient, not the last. If the egg is off or you get bits of shell in the shaker, you won't waste any spirits that way.

When you shake the drink, you're emulsifying the egg so as not to leave any, well, *eggy* bits behind. For single-serve Eggnog made in a shaker, that means putting some effort into your shake. Get some muscle behind it! Shake the drink once, hard, without ice, then shake with ice again. For batch recipes, a blender or food processor does the work for you.

HOLLY AND THE BERRY

Fruity Eggnog, why not? Blackberry liqueur (crème de mûre) adds a fun dimension to this otherwise traditional Eggnog. In the place of this liqueur, Chambord or Cassis work great, too.

1 large egg

1½ ounces Bourbon

½ ounce blackberry liqueur

1 ounce half-and-half

1 ounce Simple Syrup
(page 255)

1 blackberry for garnish

Freshly grated nutmeg for
garnish

In a cocktail shaker, add the egg and then the rest of the ingredients. Shake hard for 15 seconds. Open the shaker, add ice, and shake again for 15 seconds. Strain into a rocks glass and garnish with a blackberry and grated nutmeg.

TIP: We love this drink as a single serving from a cocktail shaker, but if you'd rather spike your premade base, add 1½ ounces Bourbon and ½ ounce berry liqueur per 3 ounces of Eggnog base (page 66).

SKINNY 'NOG

Traditional Eggnog doesn't exactly go light on the calories (or the stomach). If you want something a little less heavy, give this recipe a try. The 2% milk subs for half-and-half, an egg white for a whole egg, and vodka rather than a weightier dark spirit. Warmly spiced bitters and nutmeg in the drink make this cocktail unmistakably Eggnog-y, despite its lighter profile.

1 large egg white

1 ounce vodka

1 ounce 2% milk

1 ounce Simple Syrup
(page 255)

⅛ teaspoon ground nutmeg

1 dash Fee Brothers Old
Fashioned Aromatic
Bitters

Freshly grated nutmeg for
garnish

To a cocktail shaker, add the egg white and then the rest of the ingredients. Shake hard for 15 seconds. Open the shaker, add ice, and shake again for 15 seconds. Strain into a rocks glass and garnish with the grated nutmeg.

EGGNOG MILKSHAKE

MAKES 1 LARGE OR 2 SMALL DRINKS

We have the lighter Skinny 'Nog (the previous recipe); now let's go the other direction. Eggnog already lies halfway to dessert, and your blender is a secret weapon in the Eggnog game, so you might as well follow the path to its logical conclusion: an Eggnog milkshake.

A base of vanilla ice cream means no need for milk, cream, or sugar. Just blend the ice cream with egg, spirit, and spices, and you're done. We prefer Bourbon, but dark rum, brandy, or any combination of the three work beautifully, too. Scale up the recipe as needed to make for a crowd.

2 large eggs

1 cup vanilla ice cream

2 ounces Bourbon

¼ teaspoon freshly ground
  nutmeg

⅛ teaspoon ground clove

In a blender, add the egg and then the rest of the ingredients. Blend until smooth and pour into rocks glasses.

TIP: Pull the ice cream from the freezer ahead of time to soften. That way, it'll incorporate more easily so you don't need to blend as long.

Aging Eggnog

As we mentioned earlier, the best Eggnog uses fresh eggs, but now we're telling you to . . . age them? Well, yes. In centuries past, aging Eggnog was a common practice, and it's resurging in popularity among the bartender set. Allowing Eggnog to rest in the fridge deepens and integrates its flavors. We've tasted a notable improvement after even a week, and we've served Eggnog made in July on Christmas Eve—to rave reviews! Some folks go further, aging even for years.

If the idea of ancient dairy gives you pause, rest assured. Alcohol does a damn good job of sterilizing bacterial contamination, the usual concern for expired dairy and eggs. A 2009 study at The Rockefeller University intentionally dosed a batch of 20% ABV Eggnog with salmonella and found that, after just 24 hours in the fridge, the alcohol had killed the bacteria. You probably don't have salmonella cultures lying around, and we definitely don't recommend going that route. But if the idea of an Eggnog that improves as it matures intrigues you, make a batch and taste it once a week. Start early, and you might find your perfect 'Nog sweet spot by the holidays. But *don't* try this with the nonalcoholic bases; the alcohol itself acts as a preservative.

6.

ESPRESSO MARTINIS

BUZZY · QUIRKY · FUN

I'd like it . . .

When does a trend become a classic? Well, 40 years after its debut, in the case of the Espresso Martini. Since then, it has become both a modern classic and a trendy drink experiencing a resurgence today. Invented in the 1980s by legendary London bartender Dick Bradsell, the Espresso Martini has become a common order at just about every cocktail bar.

Made with vodka, coffee liqueur, and a shot of real espresso, its caffeinated hit delivers a buzz in more than one sense of the word.

On the sweeter side, Bradsell's version calls for rum-based Kahlúa. You can find dozens of coffee liqueurs on the market today. While Kahlúa works well in some contexts, in others we prefer Galliano Ristretto espresso liqueur, from Italy, or Mr. Black Cold Brew Coffee Liqueur, made in Australia.

The one-two punch of vodka and espresso has an efficient, undeniable appeal. But the drink's template also gives you plenty of room to experiment: with Cognac or dark rum, spiced liqueurs, even flavored whipped cream. If you're making such an indulgent drink, you might as well go all the way, right?

OUR FAVORITE
ESPRESSO MARTINI

Of all the coffee liqueurs out there, Galliano Ristretto has the boldest espresso flavor. It is distinct from a cold brew flavor; a coffee flavor, generally; or rummy Kahlúa. A cocktail bar would make this drink with a fresh shot pulled from a restaurant-grade espresso machine. At home? If you have an espresso machine or a close cousin, such as a Nespresso, that's your best bet. If not, order a few shots of unsweetened espresso to go from your nearest café. It'll keep for a few hours without losing too much flavor, and you'll shake the drink, which will revive its frothy head. Coffee beans for garnish aren't mandatory, but don't they look great?

1 ounce vodka

1 ounce espresso

¾ ounce Galliano Ristretto

¼ ounce Simple Syrup
   (page 255)

3 coffee beans for garnish

In a cocktail shaker, combine all the ingredients. Fill the shaker with ice and seal it. Shake vigorously for 15 seconds and double strain into a chilled coupe. Garnish with the coffee beans.

THE RARE MARTINI THAT'S SHAKEN, NOT STIRRED

When making cocktails, if a drink contains citrus, cream, or egg, you shake it. If not, you stir. The Espresso Martini represents a rare exception. Shaking the drink is essential for the rich, frothy head that makes this cocktail such a looker. Think of it as waking up the espresso.

IRISH COFFEE MARTINI

Irish Coffee, meet Espresso Martini. This drink incorporates the rich flavor of Irish whiskey into an icy cocktail. Going for coffee flavor here, rather than espresso, you'll use both cold brew concentrate, available at most grocery stores, and the excellent Mr. Black cold brew coffee liqueur. A thin layer of lightly whipped cream completes the indulgence.

1½ ounces Irish whiskey

½ ounce cold brew concentrate

½ ounce Mr. Black Cold Brew Coffee Liqueur

½ ounce Simple Syrup (page 255)

Cocktail Shaker Whipping Cream for garnish (recipe follows)

In a cocktail shaker, combine all the ingredients. Fill the shaker with ice and seal it. Shake vigorously for 15 seconds and double strain into a chilled coupe. Garnish with a thin float of whipping cream.

Cocktail Shaker Whipping Cream

If you're envisioning an aerosol confection atop a giant martini glass, that's not what you're going for here. Instead, you're making a rich, slightly aerated cream that gives you a pleasant float atop a cocktail. You can use one of two methods.

Into a chilled metal bowl, pour 2 ounces of heavy whipping cream and whisk until it slightly thickens.

Alternatively, use the bar method. Pop the spring off a Hawthorne strainer. Into a cocktail shaker, pour 2 ounces of cream and add the strainer spring. Seal the shaker and shake hard for 10 seconds. The spring acts as a whisk, whipping the cream just enough. This method makes enough to top 1 drink, poured right from the tin, or 2 if you scrape the sides to get all the cream. To make allspice whipped cream for the Lucky Devil (page 78), add ¾ teaspoon of allspice dram before shaking.

LUCKY DEVIL

For a switch, here you swap coffee liqueur for the deeply flavored allspice dram while keeping the coffee itself in the drink. This powerful drink tastes rich with warm spice, but not sweet in the slightest, and it stands up nicely to the allspice whipped cream.

1½ ounces vodka

½ ounce cold brew concentrate

½ ounce allspice dram

½ ounce Simple Syrup (page 255)

Allspice whipping cream for garnish (page 77)

Freshly grated nutmeg for garnish

In a cocktail shaker, combine all the ingredients except the whipping cream. Fill the shaker with ice and seal it. Shake vigorously for 15 seconds and double strain into a chilled coupe. Garnish with a float of allspice whipping cream and freshly grated nutmeg.

CORDON ROUGE

This elegant sipper makes a perfect nightcap. Try it after a holiday feast, perhaps? We recommend using a VSOP Cognac here.

1 ounce Cognac

1 ounce Grand Marnier

½ ounce espresso

½ ounce Simple Syrup (page 255)

1 orange peel for garnish

In a cocktail shaker, combine all the ingredients. Fill the shaker with ice and seal it. Shake vigorously for 15 seconds and double strain into a chilled coupe. Express a 3-inch strip of orange peel, skin side down, over the surface of the drink, run the skin around the rim of the glass to distribute the citrus oils, and add the peel, skin side up, to the cocktail.

ESPRESSO MAR-TEA-NI

A well-made liqueur is a flavor powerhouse, and Somrus Chai Cream Liqueur is a winner: vibrant, creamy, and intricately flavored. Pair it with espresso for a cocktail with layer on layer of warm spice and the buzzy energy of a classic Espresso Martini. A version of this drink spent a holiday season on the menu of a popular New England cocktail bar, and it sold so well that they couldn't keep Somrus in stock!

1½ ounces vodka

1 ounce espresso

½ ounce Somrus Chai Cream Liqueur

½ ounce Simple Syrup (page 255)

Ground cinnamon for garnish

In a cocktail shaker, combine all the ingredients. Fill the shaker with ice and seal it. Shake vigorously for 15 seconds and double strain into a chilled coupe. Garnish with a sprinkle of ground cinnamon.

BUY THIS BOTTLE

Somrus Chai Cream Liqueur

¡DALE!

Make this cocktail when you need rum and coffee simultaneously. Kahlúa tastes delicious, but its sweet rum notes run strong, making it a perfect fit for this Caribbean-inspired drink with condensed milk and a good hit of espresso over crushed ice. It's the iced latte umbrella drink you never knew you wanted.

1½ ounces dark rum

½ ounce Kahlúa

1 ounce espresso

1 tablespoon condensed milk

Freshly ground nutmeg for garnish

In a cocktail shaker, combine all the ingredients. Fill the shaker with ice and seal it. Shake vigorously for 15 seconds and strain into a Collins glass filled with crushed or nugget ice. Garnish with a dusting of ground nutmeg. Serve with a straw and a cocktail umbrella.

7.

FRENCH 75s

ELEGANT · ESTEEMED · EFFERVESCENT

Let's have a French 75 . . .

Playful and refined, this Prohibition-era favorite of Champagne, gin, and lemon juice—named for the French Army's powerful artillery piece used in World War I—is essentially a Tom Collins with sparkling wine in place of club soda. Popular enough by 1930 to have earned a mention in the influential *Savoy Cocktail Book*, the French 75 very much resembled a Collins at first, served over ice in a tall glass. But more than one version has some claim to orthodoxy.

At legendary New Orleans establishment Arnaud's French 75 Bar—which didn't invent the drink but has done more than any other venue to secure its legacy—the French 75 contains Cognac, which, unlike gin, has the distinction of being exclusively French. Arnaud's serves it in a flute, but a coupe makes an equally elegant presentation.

Some versions of the French 75 can be quite alcoholic, containing 2 ounces of spirit with just a splash of Champagne, in what essentially becomes a gin sour. Others hold back on the gin in favor of a bigger pour of bubbles. We prefer the latter approach, particularly when incorporating other flavors. Drink this bright and sparkly cocktail for any occasion: New Year's Eve, a birthday gathering, or a sufficiently festive cocktail party. Even people who don't love gin might find themselves succumbing to the wiles of a 75.

BUY THESE BOTTLES

Use a classic London dry gin such as Beefeater. For bubbles, go French but for good value steer clear of Champagne. Instead, a sparkling wine such as a Crémant d'Alsace—made the same way as Champagne but from a different region—does nicely. Lucien Albrecht is a widely available label.

ON GLASSWARE

Bartenders served the first French 75s in Collins glasses, Arnaud's French 75 Bar opts for a flute, and many cocktail bars use a coupe. What gives? Well, each glass yields a slightly different effect. A flute gives you all the fun of a glass designed for bubbly, but it can't hold much garnish. (You can't wedge a lemon wheel into one.) A Collins glass filled with ice will keep your drink colder for longer, and a coupe looks so darn classy. We pair each of our cocktails with the glass that we think most suits it, but feel free to mix it up with what you have on hand.

OUR FRENCH 75

Our preferred balance goes a little lighter on gin but big on bubbles.

~~~~~~

1 ounce gin

½ ounce lemon juice

**½ ounce Simple Syrup
(page 255)**

1 dash orange bitters

3 ounces sparkling wine

1 lemon peel for garnish

In a cocktail shaker, combine all the ingredients except the sparkling wine. Fill the shaker with ice and seal it. Shake vigorously for 15 seconds and strain into a chilled coupe. Top with the sparkling wine. Express a 3-inch strip of lemon peel, skin side down, over the surface of the drink, run the skin around the rim of the glass to distribute the citrus oils, and add the peel, skin side up, to the cocktail.

COGNAC 75

The Cognac version of the French 75 has nearly as much history as the original. No gin here; instead, French brandy from the municipality of Cognac. We love both versions equally.

~~~~~~

1 ounce Cognac

½ ounce lemon juice

**½ ounce Simple Syrup
(page 255)**

1 dash orange bitters

3 ounces sparkling wine

1 lemon peel for garnish

In a cocktail shaker, combine all the ingredients except the sparkling wine. Fill the shaker with ice and seal it. Shake vigorously for 15 seconds and strain into a chilled flute. Top with sparkling wine. Express a 1-inch round of lemon peel, skin side down, over the surface of the drink, then discard.

CUCUMBER 75

Cooling cucumber juice pairs beautifully with gin and lemon for a light, dynamic drink perfectly suited to a warm afternoon.

1 ounce gin

1 ounce Cucumber Juice (page 260)

½ ounce lemon juice

½ ounce Simple Syrup (page 255)

2 ounces sparkling wine

1 cucumber spear for garnish

1 lemon wheel for garnish

In a cocktail shaker, combine all the ingredients except the sparkling wine. Fill the shaker with ice and seal it. Shake vigorously for 15 seconds and strain into a Collins glass filled with ice. Top with sparkling wine and stir gently and briefly. Garnish with a thin cucumber spear and a thin lemon wheel.

NOTE: The flavor of cucumber juice degrades quickly. Use it the day you make it.

MINT CONDITION

Every herbal flavor takes well to gin. Making mint syrup in advance allows you to shake up a single drink at a time or make a whole batch for a party.

1 ounce gin

¾ ounce Mint Syrup (page 257)

½ ounce lemon juice

2½ ounces sparkling wine

1 sprig mint for garnish

In a cocktail shaker, combine all the ingredients except the sparkling wine. Fill the shaker with ice and seal it. Shake vigorously for 15 seconds and strain into a Collins glass filled with ice. Top with sparkling wine and stir gently and briefly. Tap the mint sprig lightly against your hand to release its aromatic oils before garnishing the glass.

WITH BELLS ON

Bold fruit flavor makes this French 75 perfect for winter, when you especially can appreciate its deep sunset color.

1 ounce gin

1 ounce blood orange juice

½ ounce 100% pomegranate juice

½ ounce Simple Syrup (page 255)

¼ ounce lemon juice

1 dash orange bitters

2 ounces sparkling wine

1 lemon wedge for garnish

In a cocktail shaker, combine all the ingredients except the sparkling wine. Fill the shaker with ice and seal it. Shake vigorously for 15 seconds and strain into a Collins glass filled with ice. Top with the sparkling wine and stir gently and briefly. Squeeze a lemon wedge into the glass and drop it in.

OUT OF OFFICE

More spirits than just gin and Cognac can go into a French 75. This drink leans tropical with white rum and guava nectar, which you can find in the juice section of most grocery stores.

1 ounce white rum

1 ounce guava nectar

½ ounce lemon juice

½ ounce Simple Syrup (page 255)

2 ounces sparkling wine

1 lemon peel for garnish

In a cocktail shaker, combine all the ingredients except the sparkling wine. Fill the shaker with ice and seal it. Shake vigorously for 15 seconds and strain into a chilled flute. Top with the sparkling wine. Express a 1-inch round of lemon peel, skin side down, over the surface of the drink, then discard.

FLOWER CHILD

The unmistakably elegant French 75 can take on delicate flavors, including rose. Too much rosewater will make a drink taste perfumy, but just the right amount yields a beautifully floral cocktail.

1 ounce gin

½ ounce lemon juice

½ ounce Simple Syrup
   (page 255)

½ teaspoon rosewater

3 ounces sparkling rosé wine

1 lemon peel for garnish

In a cocktail shaker, combine all the ingredients except the sparkling rosé wine. Fill the shaker with ice and seal it. Shake vigorously for 15 seconds and strain into a chilled flute. Top with the sparkling rosé wine. Express a 1-inch round of lemon peel, skin side down, over the surface of the drink, then discard.

Sparkling Cocktails for Parties

BATCH IT

When entertaining, we nearly always serve sparkling cocktails. To batch a bubbly drink effectively, combine everything *but* the sparkling wine ahead of time. We call it the "batch and bubble."

First, do the math. Scale up the recipe according to the number of drinks you want. Batch all the ingredients, *other* than the bubbles, along with 1 ounce of water per drink, which replicates the ice melt from shaking. Pour the batch into a watertight, quart container and refrigerate until ready to serve. Get your sparkling wine nice and cold, too.

When it's time to pour a drink? Shake that batch hard, right in the container, to remix it. Divide it equally among the glasses, top with the bubbles, garnish, and serve. We recommend measuring your sparkling wine, but in a pinch, eyeballing is OK, too. Coming in a little over or under with the bubbles won't ruin the drink. One bottle of sparkling wine makes six to eight cocktails, depending on the recipe.

Headed to a party that someone else is throwing? Bag up that quart container of batch and a bottle of bubbles, and you instantly will be the most popular guest.

Bienville

BIENVILLE

This bolder version of a Cognac 75 takes a floral hint from St-Germain and elusive anise notes from Peychaud's bitters. Complex and worth savoring, it's an after-dinner drink for sure.

1 ounce Cognac

¾ ounce St-Germain
elderflower liqueur

½ ounce lemon juice

¼ ounce Honey Syrup
(page 255)

3 dashes Peychaud's bitters

2½ ounces sparkling wine

1 lemon peel for garnish

In a cocktail shaker, combine all the ingredients except the sparkling wine. Fill the shaker with ice and seal it. Shake vigorously for 15 seconds and strain into a chilled coupe. Top with sparkling wine. Express a 3-inch strip of lemon peel, skin side down, over the surface of the drink, run the skin around the rim of the glass to distribute the citrus oils, and add the peel, skin side up, to the cocktail.

ORCHARD 75

Cognac, a grape brandy, makes a beautiful French 75, and so does American apple brandy. Rosemary honey amplifies its autumnal flavor. As always, we recommend Laird's Applejack, New Jersey's finest.

1 ounce applejack

½ ounce lemon juice

½ ounce Rosemary Honey
(page 256)

3 ounces sparkling wine

1 sprig rosemary for garnish

In a cocktail shaker, combine all the ingredients except the sparkling wine. Fill the shaker with ice and seal it. Shake vigorously for 15 seconds and strain into a chilled flute. Top with the sparkling wine. Clap a fresh rosemary sprig between your hands to release its essential oils and lay it across the mouth of the flute.

8.

GIMLETS

SMART · SNAPPY · SPIRITED

I'd like a Gimlet . . .

Order a Gimlet at a cocktail bar today, and you'll likely receive a shaken drink of gin, lime juice, and sugar. This fresh Gimlet shares a basic structure with the sour family—Daiquirís, Margaritas, Sidecars, Whiskey Sours—and has a tart, punchy appeal.

But the historical Gimlet contained no lime juice at all—rather, it contained Rose's Lime Cordial, the ancestor of the product still sold at just about every liquor store today. In 1867, to stave off scurvy, Britain's Parliament passed the Merchant Shipping Act, which required all British ships to carry lime juice for their crew.

That same year, Lauchlan Rose received a patent for the process he developed for preserving lime juice, which he called Rose's Lime Cordial, a far more convenient option for long passages than carrying fresh limes prone to spoilage. Given the officer class's penchant for gin, it's little surprise that the spirit and Rose's found their way together. By the time the Gimlet appeared in the cocktail books of the 1920s, it stood well-established in popular culture.

So . . . Rose's. Based on corn syrup, the modern version tastes sweet, kind of like puckery lime-flavored candy. In the intervening centuries, the world has come a long way, and the Gimlet has evolved with it. We no longer need citrus supplements to ward off scurvy, we no longer need to preserve lime juice without refrigeration, and fresh limes are ubiquitous, so there's no reason *not* to use fresh lime juice in your Gimlet. Essentially a gin Daiquirí, it's a bright, lively drink that's easy to love.

Like the Martini, gin is the classic choice for a Gimlet, but a vodka Gimlet tastes great, too. The Gimlet template is versatile; pair it with Thai basil and blackberry jam, blood orange juice and grapefruit liqueur, even fresh sugar snap peas and arugula. In homage to its history, we even have devised a lime syrup (known as an *oleo saccharum*) of our own (page 259).

BUY THESE BOTTLES

Use a classic London dry gin, such as Beefeater or, slightly lower proof, Plymouth.

OUR CLASSIC GIMLET

With all respect to history, we'll take fresh lime juice over Rose's any day.

2 ounces gin

1 ounce lime juice

¾ ounce Simple Syrup
   (page 255)

1 lime wheel for garnish

In a cocktail shaker, combine all the ingredients. Fill the shaker with ice and seal it. Shake vigorously for 15 seconds and double strain into a chilled coupe. Garnish with a very thin lime wheel floated in the drink.

VODKA GIMLET

Prefer vodka to gin? Go for it.

2 ounces vodka

1 ounce lime juice

¾ ounce Simple Syrup
   (page 255)

1 lime wheel for garnish

In a cocktail shaker, combine all the ingredients. Fill the shaker with ice and seal it. Shake vigorously for 15 seconds and double strain into a chilled coupe. Garnish with a very thin lime wheel floated in the drink.

BATCH IT

For 6 drinks, combine 12 ounces gin or vodka, 6 ounces lime juice, 4½ ounces simple syrup, and 6 ounces water in a quart container with a watertight lid. Refrigerate until ready to serve. To serve, shake the container hard to combine the ingredients. Divide equally among six chilled coupes, just under 5 ounces per glass, and garnish each with a thin lime wheel.

HMS *GIMLET*

This drink nods to the original Gimlet, not with Rose's but a kind of lime syrup: a citrus-based sweetener called oleo saccharum, which incorporates flavorful citrus oils from the lime rind. The addition of lemongrass and Thai lime leaf makes this drink as well-traveled as the Royal Navy. Go for Plymouth gin here, given its long association with seafaring Brits.

2 ounces gin

¾ ounce lime juice

¾ ounce Thai Lime–
Lemongrass Oleo
Saccharum (page 259)

1 Thai lime leaf for garnish

In a cocktail shaker, combine all the ingredients. Fill the shaker with ice and seal it. Shake vigorously for 15 seconds and double strain into a chilled coupe. Clap the Thai lime leaf between your hands before adding to the drink.

TIP: Tanqueray Rangpur, flavored with rangpur limes, makes this drink even more extraordinary. Keep the gin at 2 ounces, the oleo saccharum at ¾ ounce, and kick up the lime juice to 1 ounce.

OLEO SACCHARUM

The name means "oil sugar," which comes pretty close to the definition, as well. A historical method of sweetening punch, "oleo," as bartenders often abbreviate it, contains sugar and oils from citrus peels. If you've zested oranges for a cake or squeezed a lemon twist on a Martini, you know that citrus oils are *intensely* flavorful in a way that complements but differs from the fruit itself. Using sugar to extract citrus oils allows you to harness their flavors right in the cocktail—a completely different effect than from citrus juice. The oils add rich body to cocktails, too.

Like other cocktail syrups, making an oleo requires a bit of forethought but no complicated ingredients or equipment. Essentially, you peel a bunch of citrus, let it hang out with granulated white sugar overnight, then use hot water to dissolve the remaining sugar, as needed. Not a lot of effort, but lots of rich, rewarding flavor.

GIN 'N' JAM

A great cocktail shortcut, jam delivers fruit and sugar in one handy jar. It goes best in drinks with strong flavors to balance that sweetness. Here, you'll use blackberry jam for a bright, summery drink that tastes boldly fruity but not overly sweet. Experiment with other jams, remembering to adjust the amount, depending on sweetness and intensity. Sometimes you can skip the double strain, but here you need to pass the drink through a fine mesh strainer to catch the seeds and other bits.

2 ounces gin

1 ounce lime juice

2 tablespoons blackberry jam

1 dash orange bitters

1 lime peel for garnish

In a cocktail shaker, combine all the ingredients. Fill the shaker with ice and seal it. Shake vigorously for up to 30 seconds because you *really* want to break up the jam and mix this drink well. Double strain into a rocks glass filled with ice. Express a 2-inch strip of lime peel, skin side down, over the surface of the drink, run the skin around the rim of the glass to distribute the citrus oils, and add the peel, skin side up, to the cocktail.

SCORPIO RISING

We love winter citrus. Blood orange makes a juicy, appealing cocktail base, particularly with Thai basil, which contributes a dry herbaceousness that pairs perfectly with gin. Don't use Italian basil, though, which lacks Thai basil's dry aromatics. If you can't find Thai basil, try mint instead.

1½ ounces gin

1 ounce blood orange juice

¾ ounce Simple Syrup (page 255)

½ ounce lemon juice

5 leaves Thai basil, torn in half just before added to shaker

1 dash orange bitters

1 blood orange wedge for garnish

1 sprig Thai basil for garnish

In a cocktail shaker, combine all the ingredients. Fill the shaker with ice and seal it. Shake vigorously for 15 seconds and double strain into a rocks glass filled with ice. Garnish with a wedge of blood orange. Lightly tap a sprig of Thai basil against your hand to release its fragrant oils before adding it to the glass.

THE APIARY

Luscious Amaro Nonino anchors this cocktail, a take on the honey-gin sour Bee's Knees. The amaro provides complexity without overwhelming the gin.

1 ounce gin

1 ounce Amaro Nonino

1 ounce lemon juice

¾ ounce Honey Syrup
  (page 255)

1 lemon peel for garnish

In a cocktail shaker, combine all the ingredients. Fill the shaker with ice and seal it. Shake vigorously for 15 seconds and double strain into a chilled coupe. Express a 3-inch strip of lemon peel, skin side down, over the surface of the drink, run the skin around the rim of the glass to distribute the citrus oils, and add the peel, skin side up, to the cocktail.

SUMMER FRIDAY

You'll find orange liqueur everywhere in the cocktail world. Grapefruit liqueur should sit alongside it, too. Its citrus flavor animates this punchy Gimlet, which has a slightly lower proof that makes it a perfect aperitif. Giffard and Combier make our favorite bottles of pamplemousse.

1 ounce gin

½ ounce pamplemousse
  liqueur

1 ounce lime juice

½ ounce Simple Syrup
  (page 255)

1 dash grapefruit bitters

1 lime peel for garnish

In a cocktail shaker, combine all the ingredients. Fill the shaker with ice and seal it. Shake vigorously for 15 seconds and double strain into a chilled coupe. Express a 2-inch strip of lime peel, skin side down, over the surface of the drink, run the skin around the rim of the glass to distribute the citrus oils, and add the peel, skin side up, to the cocktail.

BATCH IT

For 6 drinks, combine 6 ounces gin, 3 ounces pamplemousse, 6 ounces lime juice, 3 ounces simple syrup, 6 dashes grapefruit bitters, and 6 ounces water in a quart container with a watertight lid. Refrigerate until ready to serve. To serve, shake the container hard to combine the ingredients. Divide equally among 6 chilled coupes, 4 ounces per glass, and garnish each with a lime twist.

ARUGULA GIMLET

Most leafy greens aren't going to find their way into a cocktail. But arugula's sharp and peppery bite melds perfectly with gin, and working with it doesn't differ from muddling mint or basil. Bonus? It's the brightest green you ever will see in a cocktail. Fresh ginger adds another element of spice.

1 piece ginger
   (approximately 1 inch
   long, ½ inch thick, 5g),
   peeled and quartered
½ cup packed arugula leaves
   (approximately 20g)
2 ounces gin
1 ounce lime juice
¾ ounce Simple Syrup
   (page 255)
1 lime wheel for garnish

In the bottom of a cocktail shaker, muddle the ginger firmly until well smashed. Add the arugula leaves and muddle further until wilted and releasing some liquid. Add all the remaining ingredients. Fill the shaker with ice and seal it. Shake vigorously for 15 seconds and double strain into a chilled coupe. Garnish with a very thin lime wheel.

GARDEN CLUB GIMLET

Think of this one as a cocktail for the farmer's market. Running fresh sugar snap peas through a juicer concentrates their flavor dramatically. Shake for a verdant cocktail that tastes of pure summer.

1 ounce gin
1 ounce Sugar Snap Pea
   Juice (page 260)
¾ ounce Simple Syrup
   (page 255)
¼ ounce lime juice
1 lime wheel for garnish
3 shelled peas for garnish

In a cocktail shaker, combine all the ingredients. Fill the shaker with ice and seal it. Shake vigorously for 15 seconds and double strain into a chilled coupe. Garnish with a very thin lime wheel. Place three peas on a cocktail pick for an additional garnish.

NOTE: ½ cup of fresh sugar snap peas yields about 1 ounce of juice. The flavor of sugar snap pea juice degrades quickly. Use it within 1 hour of making it.

9.

HOT TODDIES

BRACING · SOOTHING · AROMATIC

Time for a Hot Toddy . . .

For nine months of the year, the notion of a Hot Toddy probably never crosses your mind. But on bitingly cold nights, nothing warms the soul quite like a toddy. Classically made with whiskey, honey, lemon, and hot water, a good toddy soothes and fortifies. With no shaking or juicing required, it's also quite simple to make.

Once you understand the template, the Hot Toddy can prove surprisingly versatile. It has familiar building blocks (spirit, sweetener, citrus) so, as long as you keep to those foundations—plus enough booze to anchor the drink and enough hot water to warm it—the possibilities are endless.

The power of hot water lets you take lots of handy shortcuts. Usually syrups from sugar, honey, or agave sweeten cocktails. Predissolving those sugars lets them integrate fully into a cold drink. But hot water renders that step unnecessary. Just stir those sweeteners in. Hardy ingredients, such as ginger or cinnamon, often need coaxing to contribute flavor to a cold cocktail, but hot water unlocks those aromatics in a toddy. Most cocktails require shaking or stirring with ice for proper dilution, but hot water provides the necessary temperature and dilution in a toddy. Make sure your water is properly hot: just off the boil, like with coffee or tea. Then pour the ingredients, give it a quick stir, and you're ready to serve.

OUR CLASSIC TODDY

For pure comfort in a glass, add a dash of Angostura for its bold warm spice.

~~~~~~

2 ounces Bourbon

1 teaspoon honey

1 dash Angostura bitters

2 ounces hot water (just off
    the boil)

1 lemon wedge for garnish

1 stick cinnamon for garnish

In a heat-safe glass, combine all the ingredients except the water. Top with the hot water and stir to combine. Squeeze a lemon wedge into the glass and drop it in and garnish with a cinnamon stick.

JACK ROSE TODDY

An early 20th-century favorite, the Jack Rose consists of applejack, grenadine, and lime. Taking inspiration from that classic, this toddy comes together easily with a healthy pour of American-made applejack, store-bought pomegranate juice, and maple syrup. It's late fall in a hearty, warming drink.

~~~~~~

1½ ounces applejack

1½ ounces pomegranate
    juice

¼ ounce 100% maple syrup

1 dash Angostura bitters

2 ounces hot water (just off
    the boil)

1 lemon wedge for garnish

1 star anise for garnish

In a heat-safe glass, combine all the ingredients except the water. Top with the hot water and stir to combine. Squeeze a lemon wedge into the glass and drop it in along with the star anise.

Jack Rose Toddy

THE COOPER'S TODDY

Islay, a small, rugged, whisky-soaked island, lies off Scotland's western coast. Single malts that hail from there aren't for the faint of heart. Brash and unpredictable, they taste of the ocean and of the peat moss used in their production. Laphroaig 10, added solo to a hot toddy, would make your eyes water (unless you're a peat head, in which case: Try it!). But cut with Amontillado Sherry, the Scotch mellows just enough, revealing rather than losing its nuanced flavors.

1 ounce Laphroaig 10 Year

1 ounce Amontillado Sherry

½ teaspoon honey

1 dash orange bitters

2 ounces hot water (just off the boil)

1 lemon wedge for garnish

3 cloves for garnish

In a heat-safe glass, combine all the ingredients except the water. Top with the hot water and stir to combine. Stud the lemon wedge with cloves, squeeze it into the glass, and drop it in.

BLACKBERRY TODDY

Dark spirits obviously play well with a Hot Toddy, but a barrel-aged gin, such as Barr Hill Tom Cat Gin, has a weighty, piney character that anchors this drink. The hot water smoothly dissolves the unexpected blackberry jam, transforming it into a fruit syrup, so the drink comes together as easily as any other toddy.

1 tablespoon blackberry jam

1 teaspoon sugar

2 ounces hot water (just off the boil)

1¼ ounces barrel-aged gin

1 lemon peel for garnish

3 lemon slices for garnish

1 sugar-dipped blackberry for garnish

In a heat-safe glass, combine the jam, sugar, and hot water. Stir well with a barspoon or small whisk to combine and dissolve the jam fully. Add the gin and stir briefly. Express a 3-inch strip of lemon peel, skin side down, over the surface of the drink, then discard. Garnish with 3 half-moon slices of lemon and a sugar-dipped blackberry on a skewer.

NONINO TODDY

Behind the bitterness of most amari—the plural of amaro, a traditional Italian bitter liqueur—lies a kaleidoscope of flavor. Generally intended for sipping neat or over ice, some amari can make for a compelling, if unorthodox, toddy base. Among our favorites is the rich and lively Amaro Nonino, gently amplified with honey, grapefruit, and clove.

2 ounces Amaro Nonino

½ teaspoon honey

2 ounces hot water (just off the boil)

1 ruby red grapefruit wedge for garnish

3 cloves for garnish

In a heat-safe glass, combine the amaro and honey. Top with the hot water and stir to combine. Stud a thin grapefruit wedge with cloves, squeeze it into the glass, and drop it in the glass.

SIDECAR TODDY

We love Cognac and orange liqueur in a classic Sidecar (page 232), and it turns out they taste awfully delicious in a hot drink, too. Go for the king of orange liqueurs, Grand Marnier, and don't forget the big squeeze of lemon.

1½ ounces Cognac

½ ounce Grand Marnier

1 teaspoon honey

1 dash Angostura bitters

2 ounces hot water (just off the boil)

1 lemon wedge for garnish

In a heat-safe glass, combine all the ingredients except the water. Top with the hot water and stir to combine. Squeeze a lemon wedge into the glass and drop it in.

10.

MAI TAIS

ESCAPIST · TRANSPORTIVE · SURPRISING

Let's make a Mai Tai . . .

Everyone has heard of a Mai Tai, but no one knows what goes in it. Widely misunderstood, it's a bold sour that people think is just a sweet fruity drink. The Mai Tai—like the tiki movement itself, of which the Mai Tai is the best-known drink—contains a tangle of contradictions but a compellingly simple heart beneath it all.

So what is a Mai Tai? More important, what isn't it? Victor Bergeron, proprietor of the Trader Vic's bar franchise that spread from California to around the world, invented the Mai Tai in 1944. (Rival tiki bar magnate Ernest Gantt, better known as Donn Beach or Donn the Beachcomber, also claims to have invented the drink, but tiki scholars have debunked his claim.) From his Oakland, California, flagship, Bergeron served the drink to a friend from Tahiti, who declared it "*mai-ta'i*," or "good." The name stuck. The original Mai Tai contained rum, lime, orange Curaçao, and orgeat. It tasted tart, boozy, and, by tiki cocktail standards, almost restrained.

In its heyday, tiki culture smashed together a broadly Polynesian vibe with rums from the Caribbean, but the Mai Tai did develop a close association with the islands of the South Pacific. The Royal Hawaiian, the famed luxury hotel in Waikiki, tapped Bergeron to create their bar menu in 1953, six years before Hawaii became a state and tourism from the mainland exploded. Tiki bars closely guarded their recipes, so when other establishments copied the Mai Tai, they couldn't duplicate it—only imitate it—which is how lesser versions of the Mai Tai multiplied. By the time the drink became an American favorite in the 1960s, no one could come to a meaningful consensus on what went into a Mai Tai, which had become a sweet riot of fruit juice and rum.

Some drinks decline over time, such as the Daiquirí's unfortunate digression into a boozy strawberry slushie or the Whiskey Sour's long, infamous dalliance with powdered sour mix. The Mai Tai uniquely deviated from its original recipe right out of the gate. Only in recent years have tiki-minded bartenders rescued this drink from the dusty anonymity of cocktail history and revived it in its original form. So let's appreciate the Mai Tai—a bold and dynamic sour with a fascinating history—on its own merits before dressing it up a bit ourselves.

OUR CLASSIC MAI TAI

Just about every kind of fruit juice has shown up in a Mai Tai, but the original contains no pineapple or orange, just lime. That sour citrus balances the drink's other vibrant flavors, including the nutty orgeat and the funky Jamaican rum. Made properly, the unusual garnish resembles a palm tree (mint) on a tropical island (upside-down lime shell).

1½ ounces Jamaican rum

¾ ounce lime juice

½ ounce orange Curaçao

½ ounce Orgeat (page 258)

¼ ounce Simple Syrup
  (page 255)

1 spent lime shell for garnish

1 sprig mint for
  garnish

In a cocktail shaker, combine all the ingredients. Add 1 cup of crushed or nugget ice. Seal the shaker, shake hard for 3 seconds, and dump the contents, ice and all, into a large rocks glass. Lightly tap a mint sprig against your hand to release its aromatic oils. Garnish with the mint sprig and the spent shell of half a lime, skin-side up.

BATCH IT

For 6 drinks, combine 9 ounces Jamaican rum, 6 ounces water, 4½ ounces lime juice, 3 ounces orange Curaçao, 3 ounces orgeat, and simple syrup in a quart container with a watertight lid. Refrigerate until ready to use.

To serve, shake the container hard to combine the ingredients. Divide among six rocks glasses filled with ice (crushed or otherwise) and garnish away.

ALL ABOUT ORGEAT

Cocktail books dating back to 1862 have called for orgeat, simply a sweet almond syrup, by name. Orgeat is the best way to integrate almond flavor into a cocktail, and it's associated most closely with the Mai Tai today. The smooth, substantial texture of orgeat gives any drink a pleasant weight.

Good commercial brands exist—we're partial to Small Hand Foods—but you can't beat the vivid flavor of homemade Orgeat (page 258). Use it to sweeten lemonade or add it to sparkling water for a dry, sophisticated soda. You can make it with other nuts, too. Pecan Orgeat (page 258) shines in a Pecan Julep (page 148) or a Pecan Old-Fashioned (page 190), and Macadamia Orgeat (page 259) stars in our Hawai'i Tai (page 111).

The World of Tiki

One of the more fascinating chapters in cocktail history, the tiki movement has all the makings of a great story—a Hollywood setting, international men of mystery, secret recipes, wealth, rivalries, intrigue—and plenty of cultural baggage, too.

You probably recognize the tropes of the tiki world: funky mugs, faux-lynesian decor, enormous rum drinks. Tiki conjured a fantasy of escapism, but it originated squarely in America. One of the founding fathers of tiki, Ernest Gantt, who later changed his name to Donn Beach, traveled extensively around the world. Opening Don the Beachcomber in Los Angeles in 1933, he pulled together various tropically inspired elements and a menu of rum-heavy cocktails. Finding himself with a hit, he soon opened more locations. Meanwhile Victor Bergeron, known as Trader Vic, began his own tiki empire in Northern California. With their chains and the endless imitators that followed them, tiki became one of the hottest trends of the midcentury.

Iconic tiki drinks, including the Zombie and the Mai Tai, proliferated. Tiki bars had a penchant for secrecy, closely guarding their recipes and even giving their syrups and mixes code names. Rivalries ran fierce, with concerns of bartender espionage commonplace. Embracing a "more is more" ethos—more rums, more fruit, more garnish—tiki always goes big.

But to call tiki "cultural appropriation" is putting it mildly. Donn, Vic, and their acolytes cast a broad, trawler-size net for what they and their American customers viewed as enticingly, tropically exotic and shoved it all under one big umbrella: Caribbean rums, sacred South Pacific cultural symbols, loosely Cantonese food, and the sexist tropes of alluring "hula girls." Appealing to a midcentury American idea of escapism—all the attraction and indulgence of a vacation without the vacation itself—tiki "culture" quickly became a Disneyfied version of a mishmashed tropical realm that exists nowhere in reality. Its architects built the fantasy without much attention to or respect for the cultures it misappropriated.

FROZEN MAI TAI

MAKES 1 LARGE OR 2 SMALL DRINKS

The escapist vibe of a Mai Tai translates perfectly to a frozen drink, which is guaranteed to put you in a tropical mindset. Think of this cocktail as a more sophisticated version of a beach resort strawberry Daiquiri, and definitely go big on the garnish. Cocktail umbrellas always work nicely with tropical drinks. Because you use a blender for this one, you need a little more juice in the mix.

1 ounce dark rum

1 ounce white rum

1 ounce pineapple juice

1 ounce Orgeat (page 258)

½ ounce orange Curaçao

½ ounce orange juice

½ ounce lime juice

½ ounce Simple Syrup
(page 255)

1 pineapple wedge for
garnish

1 half-moon orange slice for
garnish

1 lime wheel for garnish

3 to 5 dashes Angostura
bitters for garnish

In a blender, combine all the ingredients and add 2 cups of ice. Blend until smooth. Pour into glass(es) of choice, garnish with the fruit, dash the bitters on top, and serve with a cocktail umbrella.

BATCH IT

For 6 drinks or 4 big ones, follow the directions above with 3 ounces dark rum, 3 ounces white rum, 3 ounces pineapple juice, 3 ounces orgeat, 1½ ounces orange Curaçao, 1½ ounces orange juice, 1½ ounces lime juice, 1½ ounces simple syrup, and 6 cups of ice. Garnish as directed above.

'80S MAI TAI

In decades past, your average Mai Tai probably contained rum and fruit juice, and more likely triple sec and amaretto rather than Curaçao and orgeat. But doing it the wrong way the right way can be good fun. Inspired by those fruitier versions of days gone by, this kitschy Mai Tai has good balance and tastes a lot less sweet.

Instead of dark rum, you can float a spiced rum on top if you like, but don't garnish with a proper cocktail cherry. You want the kind of neon red maraschino monster that goes in a Shirley Temple. As for grenadine? You can make your own, as cross-referenced below, or use a good store-bought brand, such as Small Hand Foods.

1 ounce white rum

1 ounce pineapple juice

½ ounce triple sec

½ ounce orange juice

½ ounce lime juice

¼ ounce amaretto

¼ ounce Grenadine (page 260)

1 ounce Myer's dark rum

1 maraschino cherry for garnish

In a cocktail shaker, combine all the ingredients except the dark rum. Fill the shaker with ice and seal it. Shake vigorously for 15 seconds and strain into a Collins glass filled with ice. Float the dark rum on top and garnish with a maraschino cherry.

BATCH IT

For 6 drinks, combine 6 ounces white rum, 6 ounces pineapple juice, 3 ounces triple sec, 3 ounces orange juice, 3 ounces lime juice, 1½ ounces amaretto, and 1½ ounces grenadine in a quart container with a watertight lid. Refrigerate until ready to use. To make two drinks at a time, pour 8 ounces of the mixture into a cocktail shaker filled with ice. Shake hard and strain into tall glasses filled with ice. Float 1 ounce of Myer's dark rum over each drink, garnish each with a maraschino cherry, and serve.

HAWAI'I TAI

Trader Vic didn't invent the Mai Tai in Hawaii, but that's where it rose to popularity. In the Aloha State, you'll find a Mai Tai on the menu at just about every restaurant, bar, and resort. Here, you'll take the tropical, refreshing character of a classic Mai Tai and introduce the distinctly Hawaiian flavors of passion fruit, locally called lilikoi, and macadamia.

Use a rich, dark rum, such as Diplomatico Reserva Exclusiva, for this recipe. Some grocery stores, particularly those with an extensive Hispanic or Caribbean section, stock passion fruit nectar—Giffard makes a delicious passion fruit liqueur. If you can find fresh passion fruit, a halved fruit makes a gorgeous garnish.

1½ ounces dark rum

¾ ounce Macadamia Orgeat (page 259)

½ ounce passion fruit liqueur

½ ounce passion fruit nectar

½ ounce lime juice

½ passion fruit or 1 lime wheel for garnish

In a cocktail shaker, combine all the ingredients. Add 1 cup of crushed or nugget ice. Seal the shaker, shake hard for 3 seconds, then dump the contents, ice and all, into a large rocks glass. Garnish with half a passion fruit or a thin lime wheel.

BATCH IT

For 6 drinks, combine 9 ounces dark rum, 4½ ounces macadamia orgeat, 3 ounces passion fruit liqueur, 3 ounces passion fruit nectar, and 3 ounces lime juice in a watertight, quart container. Refrigerate until ready to use. To make two drinks at a time, pour 8 ounces of the mixture into a cocktail shaker filled with ice. Shake hard and strain into rocks glasses filled with ice. Garnish as directed above.

FREAKY TIKI

Here, the best-known tiki cocktail goes even deeper into tiki territory. Tiki's all about excess, after all. Velvet Falernum Liqueur, a Caribbean cocktail syrup made of almonds, cloves, and ginger, takes the place of orgeat. White grapefruit and cinnamon recall the flavors of "Don's Mix," one of the (formerly) secret ingredients in a Zombie. Two rums and a little absinthe ensure that this cocktail drinks tiki-boozy. Serve in a tall glass or, if you have one, a tiki mug.

If you have a dropper bottle, that's a great way to float the absinthe on this drink. If not, pour a little bit of absinthe into your barspoon, then slowly tilt it over your cocktail, letting one drip drop at a time.

1 ounce dark rum

½ ounce Appleton Estate
   12 Year

½ ounce Velvet Falernum
   Liqueur

½ ounce lime juice

½ ounce white grapefruit
   juice

¼ ounce Cinnamon Syrup
   (page 256)

¼ ounce Grenadine
   (page 260)

1 dash Angostura bitters,
   plus more to float

3 drops absinthe

1 sprig mint for garnish

In a cocktail shaker, combine all the ingredients except the absinthe. Fill the shaker with ice and seal it. Shake vigorously for 15 seconds and strain into a Collins glass filled with crushed or nugget ice. Add more bitters to float, drop the absinthe drips on top, and lightly tap a mint sprig against your hand to release its fragrant oils before adding it to the glass.

11.

MANHATTANS

STRONG · CONFIDENT · CLASSIC

I'd like a Manhattan . . .

Less well-known than the Old-Fashioned and not as iconic as the Martini, the Manhattan nonetheless reigns as one of the cocktail world's true classics. It's a refined, spirited, beautifully balanced cocktail for whiskey lovers.

Like many other classics, its precise origin story remains shrouded in mystery. It appeared on bar and restaurant menus in the 1860s, when a bartender named George Black most likely invented it at a drinking establishment in Manhattan, near Broadway and Houston Street. By the 1880s, recipes for it made their way into cocktail guides, and its fame grew from there.

What distinguishes a Manhattan from the earlier Old-Fashioned, which it supplanted in popularity for a time, is sweet vermouth, which lowers the proof and increases the complexity of the drink. Many successive drinks eventually followed the vermouth path, including the Martini, but unlike a Martini, vermouth is nonnegotiable. The Manhattan is also one of the easiest cocktails to make: whiskey, vermouth, bitters, ice, stir, strain, garnish, done. No syrups, no muddling, no juicing.

As with any fundamentally simple drink, the details matter. Use a good rye or Bourbon. Use fresh vermouth. Bitters aren't optional. Once you've mastered the classic, it's time to branch out. Vibrant fruit liqueurs, complex *amari,* and even other spirits, such as Tequila, can find their way into a Manhattan. Want to make a round of them for a party? We've got you covered for that, too.

BUY THESE BOTTLES

Unless otherwise stated, we recommend Rittenhouse for a rye, which is affordable, widely available, and 100 proof, right where you want it for this cocktail. If you prefer Bourbon, go for Old Forester or another classic at 86 proof.

Vermouth is undergoing a bit of a renaissance lately, and you can find many excellent brands on the market. We gravitate toward Carpano Antica Formula, the gold standard, or Dolin Rouge. If you have a fancy liquor store near you, ask for their favorite; they may combust with excitement that someone actually wants to talk about vermouth.

OUR CLASSIC MANHATTAN

Two parts whiskey to one part sweet vermouth, that's all you have to remember. We enjoy the elegance of a Manhattan served up, in a coupe. If you prefer it on the rocks, that works, too. (We serve some of our riffs that have more intense ingredients on the rocks to let the flavors mingle with ice as we sip.) You can skip the cherry, but it does look awfully dashing: either on the end of a cocktail pick placed in the glass or without the pick, nestled at the bottom of the drink.

2 ounces rye

1 ounce sweet vermouth

1 dash Angostura bitters

1 lemon peel for garnish

1 cocktail cherry for garnish
   (optional)

In a mixing glass, combine all the ingredients. Fill the mixing glass three-quarters full of ice. Stir for 30 seconds and strain into a chilled coupe. Express a 3-inch strip of lemon peel, skin side down, over the surface of the drink, run the skin around the rim of the glass to distribute the citrus oils, and add the peel, skin side up, to the cocktail. Add a cocktail cherry as well, if you like.

DASH WITH CONFIDENCE

Like many classics, the Manhattan calls for bitters. Recipes measure bitters in dashes, but how exactly do you dash? Don't dribble a drop of bitters carefully into your mixing glass. Do it with gusto! Grip the bottle firmly, invert it quickly over the mixing glass, and, as you do so, give it a strong shake. A bold dash is a good dash.

All about Vermouth

Many home bartenders find vermouth intimidating or off-putting usually because of unfamiliarity or a bad experience in the past. If you read "vermouth" and want to skip to the next chapter, give us a moment to try to change your mind.

Vermouth is just wine. Producers aromatize it, meaning quite literally that they make it aromatic by steeping various herbs and spices in it. They also fortify it, meaning they add distilled alcohol to it. So vermouth is simply flavored, boozier wine. That doesn't sound so bad, does it?

Here's the thing. Because vermouth has a wine base, it starts to deteriorate once opened. If you've tasted only a dusty bottle of vermouth from your parents' liquor cabinet, we ask you: If a half-empty bottle of white wine sits on a shelf for *years*, how good would that wine taste? Exactly.

Unless you already know proper vermouth maintenance, treat yourself to a new bottle before making your next Manhattan. If you don't anticipate using it often, many brands come in half bottles, 375ml. After you open it, *always* store vermouth in the fridge. It'll last at least a few months without a serious decline in flavor—but it won't last indefinitely.

On Cherries

Everyone recognizes maraschino cherries, those neon red, chewy garnishes made for ice cream sundaes and Shirley Temples. But the word *maraschino* for those bright red monsters is something of a misnomer. In the 1800s, producers often jarred cherries in alcohol, particularly maraschino liqueur, distilled from marasca cherries. (*Marasca* ultimately derives from *amaro*, Italian for "bitter.") By the 1880s, cherries preserved in other spirits arrived in American markets, and New York City's turn-of-the-century cocktail culture made liberal use of cherries in Manhattans. Prohibition, which temporarily halted the legal market for these booze-soaked fruits, prompted the development of a method for preserving the fruit in sugar syrup. Those sugary cherries took off, while retaining the maraschino name, despite involving no cherry liqueur.

For cocktails today, steer clear of the bright red guys except for drinks with a clear sense of humor. We highly recommend cocktail cherries made by Luxardo, the Italian producer that specializes in maraschino liqueur. Though not preserved in alcohol, their cherries taste plump, dark, and infinitely more flavorful. A Luxardo or Amarena cherry garnish unmistakably signals a classy classic cocktail. You can find great American brands as well, such as Bada Bing Cherries from the Pacific Northwest. Whatever you choose, avoid cherries with colors not found in nature.

OUR BEST MANHATTAN

The classic Manhattan recipe needs no improvement, but it's fun to play with it a bit. We do like to tinker. Combining a classic Bourbon and a spicy rye achieves a lovely balance, as does pairing a richer, weightier vermouth and a bright, lively one. We'd serve this split-base recipe at a cocktail bar. Big lemon twist, please.

1 ounce Old Forester Bourbon

1 ounce Rittenhouse rye

½ ounce Carpano Antica Formula

½ ounce Dolin Rouge

1 dash Angostura bitters

1 lemon peel for garnish

1 cocktail cherry for garnish (optional)

In a mixing glass, combine all the ingredients. Fill the mixing glass three-quarters full of ice. Stir for 30 seconds and strain into a rocks glass filled with ice. Express a 3-inch strip of lemon peel, skin side down, over the surface of the drink, run the skin around the rim of the glass to distribute the citrus oils, and add the peel, skin side up, to the cocktail. Add a cocktail cherry if you like.

UN PETIT MANHATTAN

A true American cocktail, the Manhattan stars rye whiskey, 19th-century New York's favorite spirit. But for this recipe, we're borrowing from the French. Cognac makes a rich, elegant base, particularly when paired with the Cognac-based orange liqueur Grand Marnier, adding a citrus lift to this drink. Simple enough to stir together in a flash, but indulgent enough for special occasions. We recommend a VSOP Cognac.

1½ ounces Cognac

¾ ounce sweet vermouth

¾ ounce Grand Marnier

1 dash orange bitters

1 orange peel for garnish

In a mixing glass, combine all the ingredients. Fill the mixing glass three-quarters full of ice. Stir for 30 seconds and strain into a chilled coupe. Express a 3-inch strip of orange peel, skin side down, over the surface of the drink, run the skin around the rim of the glass to distribute the citrus oils, and add the peel, skin side up, to the cocktail.

FOGGY DEW

We could drink the phenomenal St. George Spiced Pear Liqueur straight, and sometimes we do. Made with ripe Bartlett pears, cinnamon, and cloves, it tastes like autumn in a glass. It also pairs well with just about every spirit, with a particular affinity for whiskey. Stirred with sweet vermouth and Irish whiskey, such as Tullamore D.E.W. (great value, widely available), it creates a riot of fall flavor against a classic Manhattan backdrop: bright, balanced, and so delicious.

1½ ounces Irish whiskey

1 ounce sweet vermouth

½ ounce St. George Spiced Pear Liqueur

1 dash Angostura bitters

1 lemon peel for garnish

In a mixing glass, combine all the ingredients. Fill the mixing glass three-quarters full of ice. Stir for 30 seconds and strain into a rocks glass filled with ice. Express a 3-inch strip of lemon peel, skin side down, over the surface of the drink, run the skin around the rim of the glass to distribute the citrus oils, and add the peel, skin side up, to the cocktail.

BUY THIS BOTTLE

St. George Spiced Pear Liqueur

PERFECT MANHATTAN

A classic Manhattan drinks bold and boozy, with a pleasant underlying sweetness to balance. The Perfect Manhattan, split between sweet and dry vermouth, tastes a touch lighter but still with all the complexity of the original. The ingredients really matter here. Use a lower-proof rye and two excellent vermouths with beautifully complimentary flavors. The big lemon twist is essential.

2 ounces Old Overholt rye

½ ounce Dolin Blanc vermouth

½ ounce Carpano Antica Formula vermouth

1 dash Angostura bitters

1 dash orange bitters

1 lemon peel for garnish

In a mixing glass, combine all the ingredients. Fill the mixing glass three-quarters full of ice. Stir for 30 seconds and strain into a chilled coupe. Express a 3-inch strip of lemon peel, skin side down, over the surface of the drink, run the skin around the rim of the glass to distribute the citrus oils, and add the peel, skin side up, to the cocktail.

CRANHATTAN

A breakout hit from our last book, Be Your Own Bartender, *this cocktail makes a perfect winter sipper. The cranberry disappears seamlessly into the whiskey and vermouth. Spicy rye and tart, dry cranberry taste perfect together, with bitters and a little sweetener to pull it all together.*

2 ounces rye

½ ounce 100% cranberry juice

½ ounce sweet vermouth

¼ ounce Simple Syrup (page 255)

2 dashes Angostura bitters

1 dash orange bitters

1 lemon peel for garnish

1 cranberry for garnish

In a mixing glass, combine all the ingredients. Fill the mixing glass three-quarters full of ice. Stir for 30 seconds and strain into a chilled coupe. Express a 3-inch strip of lemon peel, skin side down, over the surface of the drink, run the skin around the rim of the glass to distribute the citrus oils, and add the peel, skin side up, to the cocktail. Garnish with a cranberry on a cocktail pick.

NOTE: Use *only* 100% cranberry juice here, rather than a cranberry blend or "cocktail," which has sweeteners. If it tastes almost too tart to drink, you've got the right stuff.

A Winter's Nap

A WINTER'S NAP

Unique in the cocktail world, Lo-Fi Gentian Amaro brings an inviting warmth to drinks, like a cozy old sweater. The orange notes of Amaro Montenegro and a good base of rye whiskey make this reasonably stiff cocktail nonetheless accessible. A star anise contributes great aromatics and makes this drink photo ready.

2 ounces rye

1 ounce Amaro Montenegro

1 ounce Lo-Fi Gentian
   Amaro (page 27)

1 orange peel for garnish

1 star anise for garnish

In a mixing glass, combine all the ingredients. Fill the mixing glass three-quarters full of ice. Stir for 30 seconds and strain into a rocks glass filled with ice. Express a 3-inch strip of orange peel, skin side down, over the surface of the drink, run the skin around the rim of the glass to distribute the citrus oils, and add the peel, skin side up, to the cocktail. Garnish with a star anise.

GUADALAJARA

Dark, brooding, and a little racy, this drink stars Tequila reposado ("rested") with Punt e Mes, an Italian vermouth with a distinctly bitter edge, and Averna, a rich amaro. Think of it as a Tequila Manhattan with a personality all its own.

1½ ounces Tequila reposado

¾ ounce Punt e Mes

¾ ounce Averna

1 dash orange bitters

1 orange peel for garnish

1 cocktail cherry for garnish

In a mixing glass, combine all the ingredients. Fill the mixing glass three-quarters full of ice. Stir for 30 seconds and strain into a chilled coupe. Express a 3-inch strip of orange peel, skin side down, over the surface of the drink, run the skin around the rim of the glass to distribute the citrus oils, and add the peel, skin side up, to the cocktail. Garnish with a cocktail cherry, on the end of a cocktail pick, placed in the glass.

NOTE: This drink nods to the Black Manhattan, the first widely known drink to swap vermouth for amaro, specifically Averna. Todd Smith invented it at Bourbon & Branch in San Francisco in 2005, before most cocktail bars had amari at their fingertips. Now a modern classic, the recipe: 2 ounces rye, 1 ounce Averna, 1 dash Angostura bitters, 1 dash orange bitters. Stir, serve up, and garnish with a cherry.

GRAPEVINE

We all know that wine comes from grapes, but so do many cocktail ingredients: vermouth, Sherry, and brandy. What grows together goes together, so these ingredients have an affinity for one another, integrating seamlessly in cocktails. Cognac makes a great choice for brandy, though other aged grape brandies also shine against vermouth and rich oloroso Sherry. The olive garnish adds a nice little hit of salinity. Nibble the olive and sip this Manhattan for something special.

2 ounces brandy

½ ounce sweet vermouth

½ ounce oloroso Sherry

2 dashes Angostura bitters

1 orange peel, for garnish

1 green cocktail olive for
    garnish

In a mixing glass, combine all the ingredients. Fill the mixing glass three-quarters full of ice. Stir for 30 seconds and strain into a chilled coupe. Express a 3-inch strip of orange peel, skin side down, over the surface of the drink, run the skin around the rim of the glass to distribute the citrus oils, and add the peel, skin side up, to the cocktail. Garnish with a cocktail olive, on the end of a cocktail pick, placed in the glass.

IL GRAN MANHATTAN

A whiskey base cut with vermouth defines the Manhattan, and that template contributes a complex array of flavors while mellowing the overall proof. Other bottles admirably achieve those goals, too, including many amari. Gran Classico starts with a sweet warmth and finishes with a razor-sharp gentian bitterness. This Manhattan is for Negroni fans.

2 ounces rye

½ ounce sweet vermouth

½ ounce Gran Classico
    amaro

1 dash Angostura bitters

1 lemon peel for garnish

In a mixing glass, combine all the ingredients. Fill the mixing glass three-quarters full of ice. Stir for 30 seconds and strain into a rocks glass filled with ice. Express a 3-inch strip of lemon peel, skin side down, over the surface of the drink, run the skin around the rim of the glass to distribute the citrus oils, and add the peel, skin side up, to the cocktail.

EVERY COCKTAIL HAS A TWIST

PARTY MANHATTANS

MAKES 6 DRINKS

The Manhattan can please a crowd—depending on your crowd, of course—but stirring them up individually can take a long time. Here's the best way to prebatch a round of Manhattans. Recipe convention doesn't include water in lists of ingredients, but we're including it here because the water is essential, replicating the ice melt from a long stir. Omit it, and the drink will taste shockingly alcoholic, not smoothly boozy, which is what you want.

12 ounces Rittenhouse rye

6 ounces sweet vermouth

6 dashes Angostura bitters

6 ounces water

6 lemon peels for garnish

6 cocktail cherries for
    garnish

In a sealable quart container or 1 liter bottle, combine all the ingredients. Store in the freezer until ready to serve.

To serve, divide the mixture equally among chilled Martini glasses or coupes, 4 ounces per glass. Express a lemon peel, skin side down, over the surface of each drink, run the skin around the rim of the glass to distribute the citrus oils, and add the peel, skin side up, to each cocktail. Garnish each with a cocktail cherry.

12.

MARGARITAS

BRIGHT · BOLD · ENERGETIC

Let's make a Margarita . . .

Odds are, you've had a few, so the Margarita needs little introduction. It gets people excited, and it can get a party going. Making a great Margarita is a life skill worth mastering because it instantly elevates your party-hosting cred. Of all cocktails, you probably have seen the most riffs on it: strawberry, pineapple, and prickly pear Margaritas at bars and restaurants. But we're going to get a lot more creative than just switching up the fruit.

The Margarita today remains the best-known example of the Daisy category of drinks, a mostly defunct subset of the sour cocktail. (*Margarita* means "daisy" in Spanish.) Now America's favorite cocktail, the Margarita's meteoric rise coincided with the expansion of Mexican cuisine in the United States in the 1960s and the decades following. The drink, in turn, drove an explosion in the market for Tequila, a mezcal specifically from the town of Tequila in Jalisco State, Mexico. Margaritas and Tequila soon became household names, and the cocktail became a popular favorite at all manner of restaurants, bars, and parties. With such popularity, it's no wonder that many unfortunate shortcuts arose, which can decrease the quality of the drink. Let's address a few common pitfalls right away.

We shouldn't need to say it, but steer clear of mixes. Few drinks illustrate the importance of fresh juice as strongly as the Margarita. Premade mixes invariably have too much sugar—well, corn syrup—and a flat lime flavor. Switch to fresh citrus, and your Margarita wakes up. It tastes bold, invigorated, alive. The other sin of Margarita mixes? All that sugar can mask the harsh flavors of subpar tequila. You don't need to shell out a ton of money for good cocktail tequila, but don't grab bottom-shelf hooch, either. Look for Tequila labeled "100% Blue Weber Agave" rather than less expensive *mixto* Tequilas, which need to contain only 51 percent agave, with the rest consisting of neutral grain spirit and caramel coloring.

A traditional Margarita contains Tequila, lime juice, and orange liqueur. In cocktail bars these days, you also find a brighter, crisper version called a Tommy's—after the San Francisco restaurant that popularized the style—which swaps orange liqueur for agave nectar. A classic Margarita made with smoky mezcal is growing in popularity, and spicy Margaritas—a frequent call at many cocktail bars even when not on the menu—are becoming a phenomenon. Frozen Margaritas are another creature entirely.

We'll cover all the classics, and from there we'll explore how lots of fruits, herbs, and spices can find a home in the Margarita, with fruity margs, smoky ones, savory ones, and oddball ones. We'll throw in a few fancy salt rims, too.

OUR CLASSIC MARGARITA

For Margaritas, use fresh juice, no exceptions! For a good orange liqueur, we're partial to Cointreau, though it does contribute a substantial amount of alcohol. Sip slowly.

2 ounces Tequila blanco

1 ounce lime juice

¾ ounce orange liqueur

1 lime wheel for garnish

In a cocktail shaker, combine all the ingredients. Fill the shaker with ice and seal it. Shake vigorously for 15 seconds and strain into a rocks glass filled with ice or double strain into a chilled coupe. Garnish with a thin lime wheel.

> **BUY THESE BOTTLES**
>
> A great Margarita starts with great Tequila, but you don't need to go top-shelf. We like Pueblo Viejo for a great value and Lunazul for an option available everywhere. For mezcal drinks, we always recommend Fidencio Clasico.

Party Margs!

BATCH IT

The Margarita makes an obvious choice for party drinks, and this chapter features lots of batch recipes. But if you're looking for a pitcher of classic margs, nothing fancy, here's your recipe. For a Tommy's Margarita, omit the orange liqueur and substitute 3 ounces light agave syrup or up to 4½ ounces if your guests like slightly sweeter drinks.

MAKES 6 DRINKS

12 ounces Tequila blanco

6 ounces lime juice

4½ ounces orange liqueur

6 lime wheels for garnish

In a watertight, quart container or 1 liter bottle, combine all the ingredients and shake hard. Into a 2-quart pitcher filled with 4 cups of ice, pour the mixture and let it sit. After 10 minutes, the drink will have chilled and diluted sufficiently. Stir well, divide equally among glasses of choice filled with more ice, and garnish with lime wheels.

To prebatch, make the mixture as above and refrigerate until ready to serve. Then shake hard again and stir over ice in the same manner.

TOMMY'S MARGARITA

Julian Bermejo of Tommy's Mexican Restaurant in San Francisco has been making his Margaritas with fresh lime juice and agave nectar since 1990, a time when sugary mixes were ubiquitous. We love the style: bright and vibrant, focusing on the pure expression of Tequila and lime. Rather than using agave nectar straight from the bottle, make a quick syrup from it, which helps it dissolve more easily in the drink.

2 ounces Tequila blanco

1 ounce lime juice

½ ounce Light Agave Syrup (page 255)

1 lime wheel for garnish

In a cocktail shaker, combine all the ingredients. Fill the shaker with ice and seal it. Shake vigorously for 15 seconds and strain into a rocks glass filled with ice or double strain into a chilled coupe. Garnish with a thin lime wheel.

The Best Juice Is Fresh Juice

The best $10 that you can spend for making cocktails at home? A hand juicer. Fresh juice is essential in any drink that calls for citrus and *especially* those with just a few ingredients, such as the Margarita. Cutting open a lemon or lime releases that fresh, sunny aroma. Bottled juice just can't compare. It's the difference between a hot, crusty loaf of sourdough straight from the oven and plastic-wrapped, shelf-stable sliced white bread. The same thing, but not at all.

There's no shortcut to making fresh citrus juice—well, other than a restaurant-grade workhorse that'll set you back hundreds of dollars and devour half your countertop. But good tools make the job a lot easier. A two-handled citrus squeezer efficiently extracts juice and holds back seeds in one go. If you entertain frequently—like, squeezing 40 limes entertaining—consider investing in a countertop citrus press.

MEZCAL MARGARITA

In this Margarita, try swapping out Tequila for smoky mezcal.

2 ounces mezcal

1 ounce lime juice

½ ounce Light Agave Syrup (page 255)

1 lime wheel for garnish

In a cocktail shaker, combine all the ingredients. Fill the shaker with ice and seal it. Shake vigorously for 15 seconds and strain into a rocks glass filled with ice or double strain into a chilled coupe. Garnish with a thin lime wheel.

SPICY MARGARITA

A rarity 10 years ago, the Spicy Margarita has become so well-established that it almost could sustain a chapter of recipes on its own. Infusing the Tequila with serrano chile—rather than muddling the hot pepper in the shaker—gives you a more consistent final product, ensuring the exact level of heat you want.

2 ounces Serrano-Infused Tequila (page 261)

1 ounce lime juice

½ ounce Light Agave Syrup (page 255)

1 lime wheel for garnish

In a cocktail shaker, combine all the ingredients. Fill the shaker with ice and seal it. Shake vigorously for 15 seconds and strain into a rocks glass filled with ice. Garnish with a lime wheel.

NOTE: Jalapeño peppers are classic for a Spicy Margarita but range from mild to fiery. Serranos have more consistent heat, making them easier to work with.

PICANTE PEPINO

It's spicy, it's cooling, it's a party Margarita. Rather than muddling, you'll use cucumber juice and infused Tequila, which means it's almost as easy to make six of these as one. Share accordingly.

1½ ounces Serrano-Infused Tequila (page 261)

1 ounce Cucumber Juice (page 260)

½ ounce lime juice

½ ounce Light Agave Syrup (page 255)

1 cucumber slice for garnish

In a cocktail shaker, combine all the ingredients. Fill the shaker with ice and seal it. Shake vigorously for 15 seconds and strain into a rocks glass filled with ice. Garnish with a thin slice of cucumber.

NOTE: Cucumber juice is easy to make in a juicer or blender (page 260), but it declines in quality rapidly. Use it the day you make it.

BATCH IT

For 6 drinks, combine 9 ounces (1 cup plus 1 ounce) serrano-infused Tequila, 6 ounces cucumber juice, 6 ounces water, 3 ounces lime juice, and 3 ounces light agave syrup in a quart container with a watertight lid or 1 liter bottle. Refrigerate until ready to serve. To serve, shake the container hard to combine the ingredients. Divide equally among six rocks glasses filled with ice, about 4½ ounces per glass, and garnish each with a thin slice of cucumber.

CURIOUS GEORGE

This cocktail will take you on a journey: the smoke of the mezcal fading to a rich banana flavor, with oloroso Sherry backing it up. It has a lot going on, but in the end, it drinks like a lightly smoky banana Margarita . . . and you want one of those, right?

1 ounce mezcal

1 ounce Giffard Banane du Bresil (page 61)

¾ ounce lime juice

¼ ounce oloroso Sherry

1 grapefruit peel for garnish

1 dehydrated banana chip for garnish (optional)

In a cocktail shaker, combine all the ingredients. Fill the shaker with ice and seal it. Shake vigorously for 15 seconds and strain into a rocks glass filled with ice. Express a 3–4-inch strip of grapefruit peel, skin side down, over the surface of the drink, run the skin around the rim of the glass to distribute the citrus oils, and add the peel, skin side up, to the cocktail. If you have one, garnish with a banana chip on a cocktail pick.

STRAWBERRY RHUBARB MARGARITA

Strawberry margs can taste overly sweet and a little one-note—but not when fresh rhubarb joins the fun. Made with a quick blender syrup, this is a perfect party drink.

1½ ounces Tequila blanco

1½ ounces Strawberry Rhubarb Blender Syrup (page 258)

½ ounce lime juice

½ ounce Light Agave Syrup (page 255)

1 strawberry, halved, for garnish

Rhubarb slices for garnish

In a cocktail shaker, combine all the ingredients. Fill the shaker with ice and seal it. Shake vigorously for 15 seconds and strain into a rocks glass filled with ice. Garnish with a halved strawberry and rhubarb slices.

BATCH IT

For 6 drinks, combine 9 ounces Tequila blanco, 9 ounces strawberry-rhubarb syrup, 6 ounces water, 3 ounces lime juice, and 3 ounces light agave syrup in a quart container with a watertight lid or 1 liter bottle. Refrigerate until ready to serve. To serve, shake the container hard to combine the ingredients. Divide equally among six rocks glasses filled with ice, about 5 ounces per glass, and garnish each with a halved strawberry and rhubarb slices.

BIRD IN AN AIRPLANE SUIT

Margaritas should taste fresh and drinkable, but you can build a lot of complexity on the template. On first sip, this cocktail drinks bright and vibrant, with layers that emerge as you continue. The Peychaud's also gives it a lovely pink hue. Intricate enough to savor, lively enough to drink like, well, a Margarita.

1½ ounces mezcal

¾ ounce lime juice

½ ounce green chartreuse

½ ounce dry Curaçao

¼ ounce Light Agave Syrup (page 255)

3 dashes Peychaud's bitters

1 orange slice for garnish

1 cocktail cherry for garnish

In a cocktail shaker, combine all the ingredients. Fill the shaker with ice and seal it. Shake vigorously for 15 seconds and strain into a rocks glass filled with ice. Garnish with a half-moon slice of orange and a cocktail cherry.

CLASSIC FROZEN MARGARITAS

MAKES 2 DRINKS

We've said it before, and we'll say it again. Fresh lime juice is key to a Margarita—even a frozen one—so don't skip it!

4 ounces Tequila blanco

3 ounces Light Agave Syrup
(page 255)

2 ounce lime juice

In a blender, combine all the ingredients and add 3 cups of ice. Blend until smooth and divide between glasses of choice to serve.

BATCH IT

For 6 drinks or 4 big ones, follow the directions above with 12 ounces Tequila blanco, 9 ounces light agave syrup, 6 ounces lime juice, and 9 cups of ice.

FROZEN PINEAPPLE CILANTRO MARGARITAS

MAKES 2 DRINKS

Cilantro itself? Polarizing. Cilantro in a Margarita? Also polarizing, but we're okay with that. In this frozen number, fresh pineapple, Jalapeño, and cilantro meld in a tart-savory slush that might expand your definition of a Margarita. When muddled, cilantro gets mushy, which makes it perfect for a blender drink.

2 ounces Tequila blanco

½ ounce lime juice

½ ounce Light Agave Syrup
(page 255)

1½ cups pineapple chunks
(approximately 250g)

3 to 5 Jalapeño pepper
slices, sliced ¼ inch thick

½ cup loosely packed
cilantro with stems
(approximately 10g)

In a blender, combine all the ingredients and blend until smooth. Add 1½ cups of ice, blend until slushy, and divide between glasses of choice.

NOTE: The amount of Jalapeño pepper in this drink determines its heat level, with 3 slices creating a mild buzz of spice and 5 something more intense. Taste test before gulping.

Frozen Honeydew Margaritas

FROZEN HONEYDEW MARGARITAS

MAKES 4 TO 6 DRINKS

Sstrawberry, pineapple, and mango often pop up in Margaritas. We're partial to honeydew, though. Using it in a frozen Margarita means no juicing. The blender does all the work. Inspired by the Mexican snack of sprinkling Tajín Clásico on fresh fruit, we're making this drink with a rim that perfectly sets off the mellow melon.

Tajín Clásico Seasoning to
    rim (optional)

6 ounces Tequila blanco

2 ounces lime juice

3 ounces Light Agave Syrup
    (page 255)

1 cup honeydew
    (approximately 150g),
    cut into chunks

1 dash orange bitters

If desired, rim glasses of choice with Tajín Clásico Seasoning (page 16). Set the prepared glasses aside. In a blender, combine all the remaining ingredients and add 6 cups of ice. Blend until slushy and divide equally among the prepared glasses.

BEERGARITA

Bud Light was onto something: You can put beer in a Margarita. Margaritas may go down easy, but they're boozy drinks. If you want something lighter, this drink of lager and Tequila—plus a little heat from spicy bitters—should do the trick.

1 cup Mexican lager

1 ounce Tequila blanco

½ ounce orange liqueur

¼ ounce Light Agave Syrup
    (page 255)

3 dashes Scrappy's Firewater
    Bitters

1 pinch salt

1 lime wedge for garnish

In a pint glass or stein filled with ice, combine all the ingredients and stir gently and briefly. Squeeze a lime wedge into the glass and drop it in.

13.

MARTINIS

TIMELESS · STYLISH · POWERFUL

I'll have a Martini . . .

Even if you don't drink Martinis, you know the classic of all classics. People who do drink them nearly always have an opinion about them. Gin or vodka, dirty, or with a twist? Every variation changes the character of the drink dramatically. If you love a wet gin Martini, then a dirty vodka Martini might turn you off, and vice versa. Cocktail purists tend to insist on a gin Martini with a twist, one of the most elegant drinks in the canon. But if you like it dirty or dry with vodka, we've got recipes for you. Life is short; drink what you like.

Here are a few tips, whatever your preferred style. Contrary to the tastes of a certain fictional British spy, Martinis always should be stirred. (Shaking results in floating ice bits and a cloudy drink.) Give them a good, long stir of 30 seconds. Ice, the magic ingredient, transforms Martinis into cocktails. If you're doing really dry Martinis—that is, with little or no vermouth—ice is one of the few ingredients, so let your spirit spend a good, long time with it. Serve them up and, our preference, in a coupe. Whatever serving vessel you select should be ice-cold, so stash it in the freezer ahead of time or fill it with ice water before you make your drink. See page 137 for more.

BUY THESE BOTTLES

For gin, we recommend the classics: Beefeater, Plymouth, Tanqueray. For vodka, Stoli and Sobieski are our standbys. Dry white vermouth, like its sweet red cousin, is undergoing a bit of a renaissance, and you can find more great brands than we can list. Dolin Blanc is an excellent go-to, but do some exploring.

OUR CLASSIC MARTINI

A well-made Martini satisfies in a way that few cocktails can. Gin balanced by dry vermouth, stirred to an icy chill, and spritzed with lemon: a perfect drink.

2 ounces gin

1 ounce dry vermouth

3 dashes orange bitters

1 lemon peel for garnish

In a mixing glass, combine all the ingredients. Fill the mixing glass three-quarters full of ice. Stir for 30 seconds and strain into a chilled coupe. Express a 3-inch strip of lemon peel, skin side down, over the surface of the drink, run the skin around the rim of the glass to distribute the citrus oils, and add the peel, skin side up, to the cocktail.

DIRTY GIBSON

A classic Gibson is just a gin Martini garnished with a cocktail onion, so why not spoon some onion brine into the drink, too?

2 ounces gin

¾ ounce dry vermouth

¼ ounce cocktail onion brine

1 cocktail onion for garnish

In a mixing glass, combine all the ingredients. Fill the mixing glass three-quarters full of ice. Stir for 30 seconds and strain into a chilled coupe or Martini glass. Garnish with the cocktail onion on a cocktail pick.

NOTE: For a classic Gibson, omit the onion brine and increase the dry vermouth to 1 ounce.

ICY VODKA MARTINI

If you want your vodka Martini really dry, you essentially are drinking cold vodka, and there's nothing wrong with that! Let's make that cold vodka as tasty as possible with a good long stir and an ice-cold glass.

3 ounces vodka

1 lemon peel for garnish

Add the vodka to a mixing glass. Fill the mixing glass three-quarters full of ice. Stir for 30 seconds, then strain into a freezer-chilled coupe. Express a 3–4-inch strip of lemon peel, skin side down, over the surface of the drink, run the skin around the rim of the glass to distribute the citrus oils, then discard.

NOTE: For the coldest Martini, stash your vodka bottle in the freezer at least 4 hours ahead of time. The low temperature will result in less ice melt, so your drink will taste stiff and chilly. Also, Horseradish-Infused Vodka (page 261) makes for an outstanding Icy Vodka Martini, as detailed here.

We Don't Love Martini Glasses

The V-shaped Martini glasses that rose to popularity in the 1990s are *enormous*: 10, 12 ounces, or more. But a proper Martini pours out around 4½ ounces, maximum. In that case, the massive glass dwarfs what looks like a small pour of a strong, ample cocktail. If you scale up the drink to match the glass, you're flirting with overindulgence, *and* your cocktail will warm to room temperature by the time you finish. Smaller Martini glasses are better, but all V-shaped glasses are prone to spillage. We strongly recommend using a coupe instead. Save those big guys for frozen cocktails. A huge Martini glass looks pretty great filled with a Frozen Honeydew Margarita (page 133), for example.

BLUE CHEESE DILL MARTINI

Time to have a little fun with this one! Blue cheese–stuffed olives often garnish Martinis, so take it one step further by infusing the blue cheese into the vodka. Well, blue cheese and dill, that is, because the herbal note balances the cheese's crazy funk. Cheese as an infusion may sound a little suspect, but it's a version of what bartenders call fatwashing. That sounds more technical, right?

2 ounces Blue Cheese and
   Dill-Infused Vodka
   (page 261)
1 ounce dry vermouth
1 green olive for garnish

In a mixing glass, combine the vodka and vermouth. Fill the mixing glass three-quarters full of ice. Stir for 30 seconds and strain into a chilled coupe. Garnish with the green olive on a toothpick. No need for a blue cheese–stuffed olive itself; the fatwashed vodka is all you need.

 BATCH IT

Make the infused vodka the night before a party, and you'll blow your friends' minds when you serve a round of 6 drinks. Combine 12 ounces blue cheese and dill–infused vodka, 6 ounces dry vermouth, and 6 ounces water in a quart container with a watertight lid or 1-liter bottle. Store in the freezer until ready to serve. To mix, stir briefly in the container or gently invert the bottle. Divide equally among chilled coupes, 4 ounces per drink, and garnish each drink with a green olive.

DIRTY MARTINI

If you have olives to garnish a Martini, you have olive brine to make it dirty. Dry vermouth rounds it out for a salty-savory cocktail that still tastes nicely balanced. Substitute gin for the vodka if you prefer.

2 ounces vodka

½ ounce dry vermouth

½ ounce olive brine

3 green olives for garnish

In a mixing glass, combine all the ingredients. Fill the mixing glass three-quarters full of ice. Stir for 30 seconds and strain into a chilled coupe. Garnish with the green olives on a cocktail pick.

FILTHY MARTINI

Really like olive brine? Pour a whole ounce in there and forget the vermouth. Substitute gin for the vodka if you like.

2 ounces vodka

1 ounce olive brine

3 green olives for garnish

In a mixing glass, combine all the ingredients. Fill the mixing glass three-quarters full of ice. Stir for 30 seconds and strain into a chilled coupe or Martini glass. Garnish with the green olives on a cocktail pick.

PICKLE HOLIDAY

Sticking with our "garnish as snack" theme, here's something new for Dirty Martini fans. The snappy brine from a jar of cornichons works beautifully to liven a vodka Martini. With all respect to dill pickles, we want cornichons in particular here for the balance of salt and acidity in their brine. Plus, the cornichons themselves are a perfectly proportioned garnish. We love the French brand Maille.

2 ounces vodka

¼ ounce dry vermouth

½ ounce cornichon brine

2 pickled cornichons for garnish

1 pickled onion (from cornichon jar) for garnish

In a mixing glass, combine all the ingredients. Fill the mixing glass three-quarters full of ice. Stir for 30 seconds and strain into a chilled coupe. Garnish with the pickled cornichons and pickled onion on a cocktail pick.

GRANDPA JACK'S MARTINI

A certain kind of grandparent has had this Martini, exactly the same way, around 5:00 PM, every evening, for a decade—or seven. Think classic here: good, old Tanqueray; a long stir; and a big twist. If it's good enough for Grandpa Jack, it's good enough for us.

3 ounces Tanqueray

1 lemon peel for garnish

Add the gin to a mixing glass. Fill the mixing glass three-quarters full of ice. Stir for 45 seconds and strain into a freezer-chilled coupe. Express a 3-inch strip of lemon peel, skin side down, over the surface of the drink, run the skin around the rim of the glass to distribute the citrus oils, then discard.

NOTE: For another Martini worthy of the Greatest Generation (or generations prior), make this a Tom Jones. Pour some dry vermouth in a mister bottle stored in your blazer pocket until Martini hour, and spritz it on top.

Pickle Holiday

HONEY, I'M HOME

Virtually any herbal flavor pairs naturally with gin. In this Martini, you don't even need to incorporate basil into the drink itself. Simply using one large leaf for garnish gives the cocktail a bright burst of basil scent, coloring your experience of the whole drink. If you can, go for classic Plymouth gin here.

2 ounces gin

½ ounce Cocchi Americano

½ ounce dry vermouth

1 dash orange bitters

1 large leaf basil for garnish

In a mixing glass, combine all the ingredients. Fill the mixing glass three-quarters full of ice. Stir for 30 seconds and strain into a chilled coupe. Clap a basil leaf between your hands to release its essential oils before adding it to the drink.

PEACHY MARTINI

We still don't love the '90s trend of calling any vodka or gin drink a 'tini, which too often, as with the Appletini, translated to bottom-shelf booze plus brightly dyed liqueurs. But this Martini truly earns the name. In the style of the classic, it tastes bold with a London dry gin, a good dry vermouth, and, something a little different, a sparing measure of peach liqueur.

2 ounces gin

½ ounce peach liqueur

½ ounce dry vermouth

1 dash orange bitters

1 orange peel for garnish

In a mixing glass, combine all the ingredients. Fill the mixing glass three-quarters full of ice. Stir for 30 seconds and strain into a chilled coupe. Express a 3–4-inch strip of orange peel, skin side down, over the surface of the drink, run the skin around the rim of the glass to distribute the citrus oils, and add the peel, skin side up, to the cocktail.

MEDITERRANEAN MARTINI

Dry and slightly savory, fino Sherry performs beautifully in a Martini. Here it joins a few of its Spanish bedfellows: excellent vermouth blanco (we love La Pivón) and the Spanish-made Gin Mare, which features bold flavors of rosemary and olive. Serve it with an anchovy-wrapped olive and, if you're feeling snacky, a plate of jamón.

2 ounces Gin Mare

½ ounce Tio Pepe fino Sherry

½ ounce Spanish vermouth blanco

1 green Spanish olive for garnish

1 white anchovy for garnish

In a mixing glass, combine all the ingredients. Fill the mixing glass three-quarters full of ice. Stir for 30 seconds and strain into a chilled coupe. Wrap the olive in the anchovy, skewer them together on a cocktail pick, and drop into the drink.

PARTY MARTINIS

MAKES 6 DRINKS

Sometimes you want one Martini; sometimes you want a whole round. Here's the best way to prebatch your Martinis. Remember, the water replicates the ice melt from stirring. It's essential! Chill your glassware and cut your lemon twists in advance, so all you need to do is pour and garnish.

12 ounces gin

6 ounces dry vermouth

18 dashes orange bitters

6 ounces water

6 lemon peels for garnish

In a quart container with a watertight lid or 1 liter bottle, combine all the ingredients. Stash in the freezer until ready to serve. Divide equally among six chilled coupes, about 4 ounces per glass. Express a 3-inch strip of lemon peel, skin side down, over the surface of each drink, run the skin around the rim of the glass to distribute the citrus oils, and add the peel, skin side up, to the cocktail.

14.

MINT JULEPS

SOUTHERN · BOOZY · FESTIVE

Let's make a Julep that's . . .

Few drinks have such close ties to an occasion as the Mint Julep to the Kentucky Derby. Each year at the Derby, attendees drink more than 120,000 of them, to say nothing of the millions consumed at bars and in homes around the country. Bourbon and mint pair best with horse racing and ostentatious hats.

In America, the Julep is as southern as it gets, but its history stretches much further back. It descends from a Persian drink called the *gulab,* containing sweetened water steeped with rose petals. By the 1600s, Europeans were using Juleps as medicinal concoctions, and by the early 1800s, they had made their way to the American South. In 1803, the first print mention of a *Mint* Julep describes it as "dram of spirituous liquor that has mint in it, taken by Virginians in the morning." Rye and rum also would have served as common bases, but the drink we know and love today stars Bourbon, the pride of Kentucky. (By law, Bourbon can be made anywhere in America.)

A simple drink, the Mint Julep has few ingredients: whiskey, mint, sugar, and ice. Because of that simplicity, every element is essential. Always use good Bourbon and always use fresh mint and plenty of it. Also treat that mint kindly (more about that later). Ice is essential in just about every cocktail, whether shaken or stirred, for chilling and dilution. But in a Julep, it's even more crucial. Juleps should contain a great mound of crushed ice. It's elegant, sure, which adds to the appeal, but critically it also melts at a good pace as you sip, mellowing a stiff pour of Bourbon into a drinkable daytime cocktail that stays chilly for a good long time.

A classic Bourbon Julep needs no improvement, but, as with horses, it's fun to see what it can do. Try adding fresh fruit or a nutty orgeat. Get a bit unorthodox with Irish whiskey or even gin and sparkling wine. Dial up the mint or swap it entirely. If muddling a dozen for your next Derby Day party sounds like too much work, we're sharing a few no-muddle, crowd-friendly tricks that we keep in our stable.

BUY THESE BOTTLES

For this drink, stick with the classics: Old Forester or the Derby's official Bourbon, Woodford Reserve.

OUR CLASSIC MINT JULEP

Raise your glass to the most refreshing cup of Bourbon that you ever did drink. If you prefer your drinks a little sweeter, increase the simple syrup to ¾ or 1 ounce.

10 leaves mint

½ ounce Simple Syrup
   (page 255)

2 ounces Bourbon

3 sprigs mint for garnish

In the bottom of a Julep cup or rocks glass, add the mint leaves and simple syrup. Gently press the mint with a muddler. Add the Bourbon and enough crushed ice to form a mound that rises over the rim. Lightly tap the mint sprigs against your hand to release their aromatic oils before adding as garnish. Serve with a short straw.

Julep Essentials

Before you start muddling, here's what you need to assemble.

Glass: A silver Julep cup makes the best vessel, but a large rocks glass will do in a pinch, as long as it gives you room for a mound of crushed ice.

Ice: If you don't have an ice maker with a "crush" setting in your fridge at home, you have a couple of options. You can source crushed, nugget, or pellet ice from someone nearby who does, a specialty maker, or even a Sonic Drive-In. You also can convert cubes to crushed ice. Pulse ice cubes in your blender, which might have a dedicated ice-crushing setting. If you go this route, briefly set the crushed ice in a mesh strainer to drain any excess water. If you want to go old-school *and* release some pent-up frustration, put a bunch of ice in a clean dish towel; grab a mallet, rolling pin, or other heavy implement; and whack away. If you ever need a gift for the cocktail nerd in your life—yourself included!—look for a Lewis bag, a canvas sack purpose-built for ice crushing, that comes with a wooden ice mallet.

Straw: These drinking utensils are optional with some drinks but mandatory for a Julep. Why? Well, it's hard to sip whiskey through all that ice without a straw. Secondly, a huge part of this cocktail lies in the aromatics, so you want a short straw that brings your nose down to all that fresh mint as you drink. A lot of Julep cups come with Julep straws, designed just for this purpose. Alternately, you can cut a paper straw to about 1 inch above the rim of the cup or glass.

DARK HORSE

Once upon a time, America preferred rum, and a good aged rum makes a smooth, compelling base for this most American of cocktails. Here you'll pair it with The King's Ginger, a particularly potent ginger liqueur. The sharp bite of the ginger offers a perfect counterpart to the herbaceous mint.

10 leaves mint

½ ounce Simple Syrup (page 255)

1 ounce dark rum

1 ounce The King's Ginger

1 dash orange bitters

3 sprigs mint for garnish

1 piece candied ginger for garnish (optional)

In the bottom of a Julep cup or rocks glass, add the mint leaves and simple syrup. Gently press the mint with a muddler. Add the remaining ingredients and enough crushed ice to form a mound that rises over the rim. Lightly tap the mint sprigs against your hand to release their aromatic oils before adding as garnish. Garnish with a piece of candied ginger on a cocktail pick, if you like, and serve with a short straw.

Working with Mint

Over-muddling the mint is the easiest way to screw up a Julep. Why? Mint is a delicate herb. If you pulverize it, you'll end up with a brown paste that quickly oxidizes and turns bitter. When you muddle, press the mint leaves *gently* against the bottom of the cup, releasing the flavorful oils without smashing too aggressively. Think *massage*, not *mash*.

Once you've got your muddling technique down, it's time to perfect your garnish. Try a little experiment with us. Take a whiff of a mint sprig, then tap it lightly against your hand a few times and sniff again. See how much stronger the mint smells? The fancy bartender word for this technique is "activation." Activating mint breaks some of the herb's cell walls and releases its aromatics.

Finally, don't just jam a few sprigs in the ice. Presentation matters, so pretend you're arranging flowers. Bunch a few sprigs together in a bouquet, with the stems tight together and the leaves beautifully arrayed.

PECAN JULEP

Want to make the Julep even more Southern? Use pecan orgeat, a nutty syrup that integrates beautifully with Bourbon. A little dusting of toasted ground pecan tops the crushed ice.

3 pecans for garnish

10 leaves mint

2 ounces Bourbon

¾ ounces Pecan Orgeat
   (page 258)

3 sprigs mint for garnish

Prepare the garnish first. Halve a few pecans, and in a small pan over medium heat, toast them until fragrant, about 3-4 minutes. Let cool for a couple of minutes and pulse them in a spice grinder or crush by hand.

To the bottom of a Julep cup or large rocks glass, add the mint leaves and ½ ounce of the Bourbon. Gently press the mint with a muddler and add the remaining Bourbon and the pecan orgeat. Add enough crushed ice to form a mound that rises over the rim. Lightly tap the three mint sprigs against your hand to release their aromatic oils before adding as garnish. Sprinkle the toasted pecan pieces over the top and serve with a short straw.

SOUTHERN BELLE

Crushed ice and fresh mint make the Julep a summer-friendly drink. But for some people, a big pour of Bourbon feels like a bit much on a hot day. Here's a lovely alternative. The gin's botanicals pair nicely with the mint's herbal qualities, and a glug of bubbles lightens the whole affair.

10 leaves mint

½ ounce Simple Syrup
   (page 255)

8 raspberries, plus 3 for
   garnish

1 ounce gin

1 ounce sparkling wine

3 sprigs mint for garnish

In the bottom of a Julep cup or rocks glass, add the mint leaves and simple syrup. Gently press the mint with a muddler. Add the raspberries and gently muddle further. Add the gin, sparkling wine, and enough crushed ice to form a mound that rises over the rim. Lightly tap the mint sprigs against your hand to release their aromatic oils before adding as garnish. Also garnish with 3 raspberries and serve with a short straw.

EVERY COCKTAIL HAS A TWIST

BRANCA JULEP

If you're a mint maniac and you've thought that the Mint Julep just doesn't taste minty enough, this drink is for you. In this recipe, you're doubling the mint and adding Branca Menta, a powerful herbal liqueur that tastes as minty as it gets. Seriously, it runs mintier than mouthwash: You'll taste it on your breath hours later. Adding ½ ounce to a Julep supercharges the flavor just enough.

20 leaves mint
½ ounce Simple Syrup
   (page 255)
1½ ounces Bourbon
½ ounce Branca Menta
3 sprigs mint for garnish

In the bottom of a Julep cup or rocks glass, add the mint leaves and simple syrup. Gently press the mint with a muddler. Add the Bourbon, Branca Menta, and enough crushed ice to form a mound that rises over the rim. Lightly tap the mint sprigs against your hand to release their aromatic oils before adding as garnish and serve with a short straw.

BASIL JULEP

You've played around with spirits, so why not the starring herb? Swapping the traditional mint for bright, aromatic basil gives this drink a fresh and vibrant energy. In place of Bourbon, use a lighter Irish whiskey, which won't overwhelm the basil's flavor.

3 leaves basil
½ ounce Honey Syrup
   (page 255)
1½ ounces Irish whiskey
1 dash Peychaud's bitters
2 sprigs basil for garnish

In the bottom of a Julep cup or rocks glass, add the basil leaves and honey syrup. Gently press the basil with a muddler. Add the whiskey, bitters, and enough crushed ice to form a mound that rises over the rim. Lightly tap the basil sprigs against your hand to release their aromatic oils before bunching them together to form a small bouquet to add as garnish. Serve with a short straw.

NO-MUDDLE JULEPS

Juleps make a wonderfully festive party drink, but they're undeniably labor intensive. You can't prebatch them, but here's a way to avoid all that muddling: Make a mint syrup ahead of time, then just combine it with Bourbon and packed ice. For the best, brightest flavored mint syrup, use fresh mint. Want a shortcut? Mint tea steeped in water and stirred with sugar makes a convincingly minty syrup, and since you're using fresh mint as the garnish, you still get its bright aromatics.

2 ounces Bourbon

¾ ounce Mint Syrup (page 257) or Mint Tea Syrup (page 257)

3 sprigs mint for garnish

In a Julep cup or rocks glass, combine the Bourbon and mint syrup and stir briefly. Add enough crushed ice to form a mound that rises over the rim. Lightly tap the mint sprigs against your hand to release their aromatic oils before adding as garnish. Serve with a short straw.

BATCH IT

For 4 drinks, you'll need 8 ounces of Bourbon and 3 ounces of mint (tea) syrup. Combine them, stir briefly, and refrigerate until ready to serve. When you're ready to serve, have lots of crushed ice and fresh mint ready to go. Divide the mixture equally among the glasses, 3 ounces each. Pack crushed ice into each glass. Lightly tap 12 mint sprigs against your hand to release their aromatic oils before adding 3 to each drink as garnish. Serve with short straws.

BLENDER JULEPS

MAKES 2 DRINKS

What's even easier than combining Bourbon with mint syrup? Tossing Bourbon and mint into a blender. A classic Julep relies on crushed ice, so there's a clear logic to refashioning it as a frozen drink. Sure, it isn't quite a Julep in a technical sense, but it is, hands down, the easiest way to whiz up something Julep-y, fast.

3 ounces Bourbon

1½ ounces Simple Syrup (page 255)

30 leaves mint

6 sprigs mint for garnish

In a blender, combine all the ingredients and add 2 cups of ice. Blend until slushy. Divide between two Julep cups or rocks glasses. Lightly tap the mint sprigs against your hand to release their aromatic oils before adding as garnish and serve with short straws.

 BATCH IT

For 6 drinks or 4 big ones, follow the directions above with 9 ounces Bourbon, 4½ ounces simple syrup, 1½ cups (13.5g) loosely packed mint leaves, and 6 cups of ice.

15.

MOJITOS

LIVELY · HERBACEOUS · REFRESHING

Grab the muddler for a Mojito that's . . .

The Mojito has two parallel histories. In Cuba, it has served as a staple drink for nearly a century, particularly for the tourists who eagerly slurp them down. In America, it experienced a huge surge of popularity in the early 2000s and still is trying to live down its reputation as a somewhat unserious cocktail. Some self-styled mixology experts might sniff at the Mojito, but life's too short for snobbery. If you hand someone a Mojito, you probably will receive a smile in return. What else should a cocktail do?

Like the Daiquirí, the Mojito likely existed in some form long before it received its name. Published references to that name date to the 1920s. By 1931, the Mojito as we know it today appeared on the menu at Sloppy Joe's Bar, a Havana bar wildly popular with American visitors. In the early 2000s, the drink suddenly became ubiquitous in the United States, shouldering out the Cosmopolitan as the must-drink cocktail of the day. Long before fresh juices and herbs became cocktail staples, bars stocked mint just for Mojitos. Various fruity versions abounded: strawberry Mojitos, mango Mojitos, Mojitos with Bacardi Limón. If you liked bright, sweet cocktails that masked the flavor of rum, that was your moment.

From that popularity—and perhaps its appeal to those who didn't like the taste of alcohol—the Mojito gained a reputation as being unsophisticated. Bartenders who resented the labor-intensive drink also might have had something to do with its change in fortunes. Its early-aughts' ubiquity also came at the expense of quality. When everyone, even the chain restaurant at your local strip mall, is muddling Mojitos—well, those Mojitos won't always taste great.

But a well-made Mojito tastes delicious, and it offers a perfect template for riffing. Other herbs, including lemon thyme or Thai basil, can slide right in, as can other citrus fruits. Kumquat? Key lime? Bring it on! When you don't load it with sugar, even fresh muddled fruit can shine in it. To us, the Mojito just isn't a Mojito without rum. With another spirit, it becomes more of a minty Collins, but if you want to try these Mojito drinks with vodka, gin, or even Tequila, have at it!

BUY THESE BOTTLES

As with our Daiquirís, we recommend Banks 5 Island Blend Rum for a great Mojito.

THE SIMPLEST MOJITO

Grab your muddler and build this drink right in the glass.

10 leaves mint

1½ ounces white rum

½ ounce lime juice

½ ounce Simple Syrup
   (page 255)

2 ounces club soda

1 sprig mint for garnish

In the bottom of a Collins glass, add the mint leaves and muddle gently. Add the remaining ingredients and ice and stir gently and briefly. Lightly tap the sprig of mint against your hand to release the aromatic oils before adding to the glass.

COCKTAIL MOJITO

Though it adds a few extra steps, muddling the mint in a cocktail shaker before a good shake and fine strain has a number of advantages: no minty bits in your teeth, no mushy herbs at the bottom of the glass, and even more vivid mint flavor.

10 leaves mint

1½ ounces white rum

½ ounce lime juice

½ ounce Simple Syrup
   (page 255)

2 ounces club soda

1 sprig mint for garnish

In the bottom of a cocktail shaker, add the mint leaves and muddle gently. Add the remaining ingredients except the club soda. Fill the shaker with ice and seal it. Shake vigorously for 15 seconds and double strain into a Collins glass filled with ice. Top with the club soda and stir gently and briefly. Lightly tap the sprig of mint against your hand to release the aromatic oils before adding to the glass.

FINE STRAIN

"Double straining" and "fine straining" are bartender lingo for the process of straining a drink through a fine mesh strainer, as well as the shaker's own strainer. In most cases, you just strain a shaken cocktail to hold back the ice in the shaker. The holes in that strainer are quite large, the better to pour the drink out. When using a second strainer, you're aiming to catch smaller bits: fruit seeds, ice chips, or, in this case, mint flecks. It's not mandatory, but a fine strain will give you a cleaner, better-looking drink (and keep those mint bits out of your teeth).

PITCHER MOJITOS

MAKES 6 DRINKS

The Mojito is inherently a party drink, but it can be a chore to make for a crowd because there's no good way to muddle more than one at a time. Our solution? Make mint syrup ahead of time. When you're ready, just pour it out with rum, lime, and soda.

9 ounces white rum

4½ ounces Mint Syrup (page 257)

4½ ounces lime juice

6 ounces water

12 ounces club soda

4 to 12 sprigs mint for garnish

In a watertight, quart container, combine all the ingredients except the club soda. Refrigerate until ready to use. To serve, shake the container hard, then pour into a pitcher filled with ice. Add the club soda and stir gently and briefly. Pour equally into four glasses filled with ice, 6 ounces per glass. Lightly tap the mint sprigs against your hand to release their aromatic oils before adding to the glasses.

MOJITO IN A MINUTE

For 1 drink, combine 1½ ounces white rum, ¾ ounce lime juice, and ¾ ounce mint syrup in a cocktail shaker. Fill the shaker with ice and seal it. Shake vigorously for 15 seconds and strain into a Collins glass filled with ice. Top with 2 ounces club soda and stir gently and briefly. Lightly tap 3 sprigs of mint against your hand to release their aromatic oils. Bundle them into a bouquet before adding them to the glass.

LA BODEGUITA

This is a culinary, California sort of Mojito. If you like messing around in the kitchen, it's definitely for you. Muddling kumquats captures their vivid, slightly floral flavor, and the dry, fragrant lemon thyme offers a powerful counterpoint.

⅓ cup (approximately 45g) fresh kumquats

1½ ounces white rum

½ ounce lime juice

½ ounce Honey Syrup (page 255)

1 tablespoon (approximately 2.5g) lemon thyme leaves

1 ounce club soda

1 kumquat, halved, for garnish

1 sprig lemon thyme for garnish

In the bottom of a cocktail shaker, muddle the kumquats firmly until the skins break up and much of the juice squeezes out. Add the remaining ingredients except the club soda. Fill the shaker with ice and seal it. Shake vigorously for 15 seconds and double strain into a Collins glass filled with ice. Top with club soda and stir gently and briefly. Garnish with the halved kumquat and the lemon thyme sprig.

TIP: With the lemon thyme, try to pick just the leaves and remove as many of the stalks and stems as you can. It's fine if some of them wind up in the shaker (because you'll strain them out), but if too many sneak in, the drink will taste woody.

FINDERS KEEPERS

Key limes, Thai basil, lemongrass—there's so much going on in this drink, but muddling the limes is key (pun intended). Rather than juicing, you're muddling the entire fruit, which allows the flavorful, complex oils in the rind to integrate into the drink. Those lime notes nicely complement the dry herbaceousness of Thai basil. Garnish with the prettiest sprig of the bunch.

3 lemongrass segments (approximately 1 inch long, 12g total)

4 key limes (approximately 70g), halved

1½ ounces white rum

¾ ounce Simple Syrup (page 255)

10 leaves Thai basil, torn in half just before adding to shaker

2 ounces club soda

½ key lime for garnish

1 large sprig Thai basil for garnish

In the bottom of a cocktail shaker, muddle the lemongrass firmly until the segments break up. Add the key lime halves and continue muddling firmly until the skins break up and much of the juice squeezes out. Add the remaining ingredients except the club soda. Fill the shaker with ice and seal it. Shake vigorously for 15 seconds and double strain into a Collins glass filled with ice. Top with club soda and stir gently and briefly. Garnish with the key lime and sprig of Thai basil.

VIBE SHIFT

When pineapple hits the grill, its sugars caramelize and deepen, and the fruit picks up a bit of smoky char. Those rich, caramelized flavors pair perfectly with rum in this tropical cocktail, and the Thai lime leaves add nuanced aromatics against the fruity background.

3 Thai lime leaves, torn in several pieces before adding to shaker

4 Grilled Pineapple chunks (approximately 1 inch cubes, 40g), recipe follows

1½ ounces white rum

½ ounce lime juice

½ ounce Raw Sugar Syrup (page 256)

2 ounces club soda

1 Thai lime leaf for garnish

1 grilled pineapple triangle chunk for garnish

In the bottom of a cocktail shaker, muddle the Thai lime leaves. Add the grilled pineapple and continue muddling firmly until much of the juice squeezes out. Add the remaining ingredients except the club soda. Fill the shaker with ice and seal it. Shake vigorously for 15 seconds and double strain into a Collins glass filled with ice. Top with the club soda and stir gently and briefly. Garnish with the Thai lime leaf and a triangle of grilled pineapple.

GRILLED PINEAPPLE

Over medium heat, grill 1-inch-thick slices of pineapple, rind removed, 3 to 5 minutes per side, until brown grill marks appear but before the fruit chars. Allow to cool for a couple of minutes, then cut into 1-inch-square chunks.

FOLLOW THE SUN

As vibrantly flavored as it is vividly colored, hibiscus (or sorrel) stars in drinks in many parts of the Caribbean, Latin America, West Africa, and beyond. In this drink, hibiscus brightens a weighty dark rum, while lime and mint contribute their signature freshness. You can find dried hibiscus flowers in many international grocery stores or online, but we often reach for Tazo Passion Herbal Tea—with hibiscus, orange peel, lemongrass, and rose hip—as a tasty shortcut.

10 leaves mint

1½ ounces dark rum

¾ ounce lime juice

¾ ounce Hibiscus Syrup
   (page 258)

2 ounces club soda

1 sprig mint for garnish

In the bottom of a cocktail shaker, gently muddle the mint leaves. Add the remaining ingredients except the club soda. Fill the shaker with ice and seal it. Shake vigorously for 15 seconds and double strain into a Collins glass filled with ice. Top with the club soda and stir gently and briefly. Lightly tap the sprig of mint against your hand to release the aromatic oils before adding to the glass.

TIP: To make this drink even more interesting, add ¾ ounce oloroso Sherry, which contributes subtle depth and character.

MR. WORLDWIDE

Havana has multiple signature drinks, with the Mojito and the Daiquirí at the top of the list. There, Habaneros usually make frozen Daiquirís with maraschino liqueur. It turns out that maraschino works mighty well in the Mojito, too. Reach for the good stuff—Luxardo Maraschino—to add a new side to one of the marquee drinks of the City of Columns. Here the mint appears only as garnish, with no muddling required. Think of this drink as beachy sophistication with a sense of humor.

2 ounces coconut LaCroix

1½ ounces white rum

¾ ounce lime juice

½ ounce Simple Syrup
(page 255)

¼ ounce Luxardo
Maraschino

1 sprig mint for garnish

In a Collins glass filled with ice, combine all the ingredients. Stir gently and briefly. Lightly tap the sprig of mint against your hand to release the aromatic oils before adding to the glass.

BATCH IT

No muddling makes this a great party drink. Scale the ingredients up, combine everything in a pitcher with lots of ice, stir well, pour over more ice, and don't forget the mint garnish. It may be offbeat, but this is a Mojito, after all.

RASPBERRY MOJITO

This cocktail may not soar to the pinnacle of modern mixology, but it is undeniably delicious. Tart, juicy berries making friends with mint and lime, what's not to like?

5 raspberries

10 leaves mint

1½ ounces white rum

¾ ounce lime juice

¾ ounce Simple Syrup
(page 255)

2 ounces club soda

1 sprig mint for garnish

3 raspberries for garnish

In the bottom of a cocktail shaker, muddle the raspberries until they break up. Add the mint leaves and muddle gently. Add the remaining ingredients except the club soda. Fill the shaker with ice and seal it. Shake vigorously for 15 seconds and double strain into a Collins glass filled with ice. Top with the club soda and stir gently and briefly. Lightly tap the sprig of mint against your hand to release the aromatic oils before adding to the glass with 3 whole raspberries.

TIP: To make this drink even more compelling, add ¾ ounce Lillet Rosé, which imparts a smooth elegance without hiding the raspberry or detracting from the cocktail's essential easy-drinking character.

FROJITOS

MAKES 2 DRINKS

Skip the muddling and grab the blender. If this drink doesn't transport you to a beachy state of mind, we don't know what will. Use white rum for classic Mojito flavor, but this recipe tastes just as delicious with dark rum, too.

3 ounces rum

2 ounces lime juice

2 ounces Raw Sugar Syrup
(page 256)

30 leaves mint (9g)

4 sprigs mint for garnish

In a blender, combine all the ingredients and add 2 cups of ice. Blend until smooth and divide between two glasses of choice. Lightly tap the mint sprigs against your hand to release their aromatic oils before adding to the glasses.

BATCH IT

For 6 drinks or 4 big ones, follow the directions as here with 9 ounces rum, 6 ounces lime juice, 6 ounces raw sugar syrup, 1½ cups mint leaves, and 6 cups of ice.

16.

MULES, STORMIES & BUCKS

FIZZY · ZINGY · VIVACIOUS

Let's have . . .

The Moscow Mule and the Dark 'n' Stormy have achieved such popularity that they could sustain chapters of their own, but, given their fundamental similarity—as members of the historical Buck category—we'll look at the family as a whole.

Let's start with basics. A classic Moscow Mule contains vodka and ginger beer, served in a copper mug, over ice, with a lime wedge. Unlike so many classics, their origins obscured by the fog of booze and time, the Mule has a documented origin story, which we'll share later. The Dark 'n' Stormy proper contains Goslings Black Seal Rum and ginger beer served over ice with a lime. In 1991, Gosling Brothers trademarked the Dark 'n' Stormy (just one apostrophe, not the grammatically correct two), which, by law, must contain Goslings Black Seal Rum, the pride of Bermuda. If companies don't defend violations of their trademarks, they lose them, so Gosling Brothers somewhat militantly guards the use of the cocktail name in relation to its

rum. So for our purposes, let's call a drink of dark rum—whatever the brand—with ginger beer and lime a Stormy. What about the Buck? It consists of any spirit served as a highball with ginger beer or ginger ale and, usually, citrus.

Taken together, Mules, Stormies & Bucks showcase ginger beer as one of the cocktail world's essentials. Mix it with just about any spirit, and you're in for something exciting. So many flavors pair nicely with ginger, so the opportunities for experimentation are endless. Whether you want a summery cherry Mule or an autumnal applejack Buck, a super-gingery Stormy, or a Mule that tastes as virtuous as a green juice, we've got a drink for you.

The History of the Moscow Mule

The origin stories of many classic cocktails lie shrouded in legend; some have conflicting backstories. A few came, documented, from the hands of a single bartender. The Moscow Mule was a pure marketing invention—and an exceptionally tasty one.

In 1939, John Martin, president of the Heublein spirits company, acquired the rights to Smirnoff vodka, which Pyotr Smirnov had founded in Moscow in 1864. At this point in history, America liked whiskey, so Heublein, Martin's company, positioned this new, unfamiliar liquor as "white whiskey." Jack Morgan, one of Martin's friends, owned the Cock'n Bull restaurant (single apostrophe again) on Sunset Boulevard in West Hollywood. Morgan had produced a spicy ginger beer that wasn't selling, and another friend of Morgan had inherited a copper goods company. In 1941, so the story goes, Martin and Morgan paired their products—vodka and ginger beer—saw the potential of a copper mug as the drink's signature vessel, and the Moscow Mule was born, its name nodding to vodka's homeland. Years later, Wes Price, Cock'n Bull's head bartender at the time, claimed that he had invented the Mule to clear out the bar's stock of ginger beer. Either way, its origins at the West Hollywood tavern are clear.

A salesman by trade, Martin spent years advocating for the drink. Using a Polaroid camera, which debuted in the late 1940s, he enlisted bartenders to pose with a copper mug in one hand and a bottle of Smirnoff in the other. Martin then left the novelty photo behind for staff to display at the bar, a decidedly pre-social-media attempt at viral marketing. Aided by such promotion in Los Angeles and beyond, the Moscow Mule's popularity spread across the country, and, with the Bloody Mary, played a major role in elevating vodka to America's number one spirit.

Why the Mug?

Apparently we all drink Moscow Mules from copper mugs because, according to the origin story, a copper heiress had product to move. But the mugs have endured, along with the drink itself, for a reason. The eye-catching copper elevates an otherwise unremarkable highball to something a little more festive. The metal also helps keep your drink icy cold. If you don't have a Mule mug handy, a Collins glass or a large rocks glass will do just fine. But we're partial to those shiny mugs.

OUR MOSCOW MULE

The original Moscow Mule has lime only as a garnish, but we greatly prefer the drink with a bit of lime juice in the glass. If you want to skip the lime juice, squeeze the garnish into the drink at the very least. Pick a mellow ginger beer if that's your style, or try something off-the-wall gingery, such as Reed's Extra Ginger Brew. Fever-Tree Ginger Beer, our go-to, lies somewhere in the middle.

4 ounces ginger beer

2 ounces vodka

½ ounce lime juice

1 lime wedge for garnish

In a mule mug or Collins glass filled with ice, combine all the ingredients. Stir gently and briefly. Squeeze the lime wedge into the glass and drop it in.

MEZCAL MULE

Smoky, multifaceted mezcal makes a great base for a refreshing Mule. We recommend Fidencio Clásico mezcal here. You'll use grapefruit and lime for the citrus element, with an unexpected ingredient to tie it all together: salt. If you like the rim of your Margarita salted, rim this drink with salt, as well.

1½ ounces mezcal

1 ounce ruby red grapefruit
    juice

½ ounce Light Agave Syrup
    (page 255)

½ ounce lime juice

1 pinch salt

2 ounces ginger beer

1 grapefruit slice for garnish

1 lime wheel for garnish

In a cocktail shaker, combine all the ingredients except the ginger beer. Fill the shaker with ice and seal it. Shake vigorously for 15 seconds and double strain into a mule mug or Collins glass filled with ice. Top with the ginger beer and stir gently and briefly. Garnish with a half-moon slice of grapefruit and the lime wheel.

BATCH IT

For 6 drinks, combine 9 ounces mezcal, 6 ounces grapefruit juice, 3 ounces light agave syrup, 3 ounces lime juice, and ⅛ teaspoon salt. Add ice and stir until well-chilled, then add 12 ounces ginger beer (usually one single-serving bottle) and stir again gently and briefly to combine ingredients. Divide equally among Collins glasses and garnish with citrus.

KIDS THESE DAYS

If you wish that most cocktails tasted a little fresher and a little less sweet, we've got you. Celery and ginger, muddled together, create a sharp, vibrant, downright virtuous backdrop for lemon and vodka. As hair of the dog, this drink is sure to expunge any sins of the night before.

1 piece peeled ginger
   (approximately 1 inch
   long, ¼ inch thick, 5g),
   cut into pieces
3 celery segments
   (approximately 2 inches
   long, 30g), cut into
   pieces
1½ ounces vodka
¾ ounce lemon juice
¾ ounce Simple Syrup
   (page 255)
2 ounces ginger beer
1 stalk celery, cut lengthwise
   into 3 thin slices, to
   garnish

In the bottom of a cocktail shaker, muddle the ginger firmly until well smashed, then add the celery and muddle again. Add the remaining ingredients except the ginger beer. Fill the shaker with ice and seal it. Shake vigorously for 15 seconds and double strain into a mule mug or Collins glass filled with ice. Top with the ginger beer and stir gently and briefly. Garnish with the stalks of celery.

VANILLA MULE

In the 1990s (at the risk of dating ourselves), Stoli Vanil and ginger ale was a popular New York club drink and, we have to admit, a pretty tasty one. Rather than buying a full bottle of overly sweet and artificial-tasting vanilla-flavored vodka, use a few drops of vanilla extract to achieve the flavor of pure '90s energy.

4 ounces ginger ale

1½ ounces vodka

3 drops vanilla extract

1 lemon wedge for garnish

In a mule mug or Collins glass filled with ice, combine all the ingredients. Stir gently and briefly. Squeeze the lemon wedge into the glass and drop it in.

CHERRY MULE

The Moscow Mule trio of vodka, lime, and ginger exhibits a perfect simplicity that also takes well to riffing. Available in most grocery stores, 100% tart cherry juice makes an ideal companion, adding a rich, summery fruit flavor to the bright, snappy ginger. You don't even have to muddle; just pour it on in.

2½ ounces ginger beer

2 ounces 100% tart cherry juice

1½ ounces vodka

¾ ounce Raw Sugar Syrup (page 256)

¼ ounce lime juice

1 dash Angostura bitters

1 lime wedge for garnish

In a mule mug or Collins glass filled with ice, combine all the ingredients. Stir gently and briefly. Squeeze the lime wedge into the glass and drop it in.

BATCH IT

A barren of Cherry Mules for brunch, perhaps? For 6 drinks, combine 12 ounces tart cherry juice, 9 ounces vodka, 4½ ounces raw sugar syrup, 1½ ounces lime juice, and 6 dashes Angostura bitters. Add ice and stir until well-chilled, then add 15 ounces ginger beer and stir again gently and briefly. Pour into Collins glasses filled with ice and garnish them with lime wedges.

DARK 'N' STORMY

You must make the Dark 'n' Stormy, one of only four internationally trademarked cocktails, with Goslings Black Seal Rum. Here's the official recipe for this sweet but undeniably tasty drink.

6 ounces Goslings Stormy
   Ginger Beer
2 ounces Goslings Black Seal
   Rum
1 lime wedge for garnish

In a Collins glass filled with ice, pour the ginger beer. Float the rum on top. Squeeze the lime wedge into the glass and drop it in.

OUR STORMY

A little more lime, a lot less sweet. We recommend Banks 7 Golden Age Rum for a great dark rum drink.

4 ounces ginger beer
2 ounces dark rum
½ ounce lime juice
Lime wedge for garnish

In a Collins glass filled with ice, combine all the ingredients. Stir gently and briefly. Squeeze the lime wedge into the glass and drop it in.

GINGER STORMY

Ginger enthusiasts will love this version, which swaps ginger beer for fresh muddled ginger. It drinks dry, spicy, and delicious.

~~~~~~

1 piece peeled ginger (approximately 1 inch long, ¼ inch thick, 4g), cut into pieces

2 ounces dark rum

1 ounce lime juice

¾ ounce Simple Syrup (page 255)

2 ounces club soda

1 lime wedge for garnish

In the bottom of a cocktail shaker, add the ginger and muddle it firmly until well smashed. Add the remaining ingredients except the club soda. Fill the shaker with ice and seal it. Shake vigorously for 15 seconds and double strain into a Collins glass filled with ice. Top with the club soda and stir gently and briefly. Squeeze the lime wedge into the glass and drop it in.

TIP: If you *really* like ginger, swap ginger beer for the club soda.

HOLLY JOLLY

Whereas some cocktails drink frosty and autumnal, this one goes all in on winter. Festive and celebratory, the cranberry, ginger, and orange recall a holiday relish or chutney. Dark rum anchors the cocktail, with bitters, nutmeg, and ginger beer providing seasonal spice. Use whatever orange liqueur you have, but Grand Marnier tastes awfully nice, especially during the holidays.

1½ ounces dark rum

¾ ounce 100% cranberry
   juice

½ ounce orange liqueur

½ ounce Raw Sugar Syrup
   (page 256)

¼ ounce lime juice

3 dashes Angostura bitters

1½ ounces ginger beer

1 lime wedge for garnish

Nutmeg for garnish

In a cocktail shaker, combine all the ingredients except the ginger beer. Fill the shaker with ice and seal it. Shake vigorously for 15 seconds and double strain into a mule mug or Collins glass filled with ice. Top with the ginger beer and stir gently and briefly. Squeeze the lime wedge into the glass and drop it in. Also garnish with freshly grated nutmeg.

BATCH IT

For 6 drinks, combine 9 ounces dark rum, 4½ ounces cranberry juice, 3 ounces orange liqueur, 3 ounces raw sugar syrup, 1½ ounces lime juice, and 18 dashes (½ ounce) Angostura bitters. Add ice and stir until well-chilled. Add 9 ounces ginger beer and stir again gently and briefly. Don't forget the fresh grated nutmeg to garnish each glass.

SHIVER ME GINGERS

MAKES 2 DRINKS

Stormies make great summer drinks, so a frozen version is a no-brainer. Spice it up (pun intended) with Kraken, our favorite spiced rum, and a whole lot of Angostura bitters. Frosty and delicious.

4 ounces Kraken Black
   Spiced Rum

2 ounces lime juice

1½ ounces Raw Sugar Syrup
   (page 256)

1 ounce Ginger Juice (page
   260)

10 dashes Angostura bitters,
   plus more for garnish

2 orange wedges for garnish

In a blender, combine all the ingredients and add 2 cups of ice. Blend until slushy and divide between two glasses of choice. Garnish each drink with additional Angostura bitters and an orange wedge. Serve with straws and, not discouraged, cocktail umbrellas.

BATCH IT

For 6 drinks, use 12 ounces Kraken Black Spiced Rum, 6 ounces lime juice, 4½ ounces raw sugar syrup, 3 ounces ginger juice, 1 ounce Angostura bitters, and 6 cups of ice. Tip: pop the dropper spout off the bottle of Angostura to pour it into your jigger.

APPLE A DAY

Ginger can pair with almost any spirit and for any season. But it has a particular affinity for whiskey. Bourbon, green apple, and honey set the stage for this warming, autumnal Buck. Don't skip a fragrant sprinkle of cinnamon on top.

¼ medium green apple
   (approximately 35g), cut
   into pieces, plus additional
   thin slices for garnish

1½ ounces Bourbon

¾ ounce lemon juice

½ ounce Honey Syrup
   (page 255)

2 dashes Angostura bitters

2 ounces ginger beer

Ground cinnamon for garnish

In the bottom of a cocktail shaker, muddle the apple pieces until they start to break up. Add the remaining ingredients except 1 dash of the bitters and the ginger beer. Fill the shaker with ice and seal it. Shake vigorously for 15 seconds and double strain into a mule mug or Collins glass filled with ice. Top with the ginger beer and stir gently and briefly. Garnish with the green apple slices, a sprinkle of ground cinnamon, and 1 dash of bitters.

EMERALD ISLE

When you're looking for a refreshing, easy-drinking whiskey cocktail, go Irish. The friendly nature of Irish whiskey pairs perfectly with basil and lemon. Make it fizzy with a good pour of ginger ale for a definite crowd pleaser.

5 leaves basil

1½ ounces Irish whiskey

¾ ounce lemon juice

½ ounce Honey Syrup (page 255)

1 dash grapefruit bitters

2 ounces ginger ale

1 sprig basil for garnish

In the bottom of a cocktail shaker, gently muddle the basil. Add the remaining ingredients except the ginger ale. Fill the shaker with ice and seal it. Shake vigorously for 15 seconds and double strain into a Collins glass filled with ice. Add the ginger ale and stir gently and briefly. Clap the basil sprig between your hands to release its essential oils before adding to the drink.

MONMOUTH BUCK

Applejack is perhaps the most underappreciated American spirit. Its history dates to the Colonial period, and the liquid has a rich character reminiscent of whiskey— if whiskey grew in an orchard, that is. This highball drinks like fall in a glass and comes together in seconds. So easy, so good.

1½ ounces applejack

4 ounces ginger ale

1 lemon wedge for garnish

1 sprig rosemary for garnish

In a mule mug or Collins glass filled with ice, combine the applejack and ginger ale. Stir gently and briefly. Squeeze the lemon wedge into the glass and drop it in. Clap the fresh rosemary sprig between your hands to release its essential oils before adding it to the drink.

BATCH IT

For 6 drinks, combine 9 ounces applejack and 24 ounces ginger ale in a pitcher filled with ice. Give it a quick and gentle stir, then pour into glasses filled with ice. Don't forget the lemon and rosemary garnishes.

17.

NEGRONIS

POLISHED · BITTER · ALLURING

I'd like a Negroni that's . . .

Many classic cocktails have American roots. Not so the Negroni. Named for Camillo Negroni—definitely Florentine, possibly a count—this cocktail gained prominence after World War II. It developed a reputation for Italian sophistication, which it retains today.

We often talk about "balance" in cocktails. Nowhere is that more important than for this one, traditionally made in a precise braiding of three equal parts: assertive gin, accommodating sweet vermouth, and capricious Campari. These create a delicate dance of strong and supple, herbal and weighty, bitter and sweet. Unapologetically itself, the Negroni has a carmine color and a sharp edge that command attention. It's not for everyone, but if you like your cocktails stiff and bitter, few drinks are more fulfilling.

Mixologists also love to play with it. You can switch out each of its elements: gin for another spirit, Campari for another bitter liqueur, sweet vermouth for Sherry, Port, or Lillet. If you enjoy the Negroni vibe but find the classic too potent, there are plenty of ways to lighten it up, as well.

BUY THESE BOTTLES

We use Beefeater, a classic London dry gin, and Carpano Antica Formula sweet vermouth. For Campari, there's no substitute.

Our Classic Negroni

OUR CLASSIC NEGRONI

The classic recipe calls for equal parts of the three main ingredients. But we consider the Negroni, at heart, a gin drink, so in our version we increase the measure of gin accordingly. The grapefruit bitters pull it all together.

1½ ounces gin

1 ounce sweet vermouth

1 ounce Campari

1 dash grapefruit bitters

1 orange peel for garnish

In a mixing glass, combine all the ingredients. Fill the mixing glass three-quarters full of ice. Stir for 30 seconds and strain into a rocks glass filled with ice. Express a 3–4-inch strip of orange peel, skin side down, over the surface of the drink, run the skin around the rim of the glass to distribute the citrus oils, and add the peel, skin side up, to the cocktail.

AMERICANO

If you like the bitter, complex union of Campari and sweet vermouth but want to go lighter on the alcohol, the Americano, another Italian classic, is for you. Have it as an aperitif to pique your appetite.

1 ounce sweet vermouth

1 ounce Campari

3 ounces club soda

1 orange slice for garnish

In a Collins glass filled with ice, combine all the ingredients, adding the club soda last. Stir gently and briefly to combine. Garnish with a thick half-moon slice of orange.

BOULEVARDIER

In this classic variation, gin simply swaps out in favor of Bourbon. The result drinks a little weightier and a little bigger, but it keeps the Negroni's signature edge. Go big on the Bourbon for this one.

2 ounces Bourbon

1 ounce sweet vermouth

1 ounce Campari

1 lemon peel for garnish

In a mixing glass, combine all the ingredients. Fill the mixing glass three-quarters full of ice. Stir for 30 seconds and strain into a rocks glass filled with ice. Express a 3-inch strip of lemon peel, skin side down, over the surface of the drink, run the skin around the rim of the glass to distribute the citrus oils, and add the peel, skin side up, to the cocktail.

NEGRONI SBAGLIATO

In Italian, sbagliato means "mistaken," and this drink reportedly came about when a busy Italian bartender grabbed Prosecco instead of gin while making a Negroni. The story feels flimsy, to say the least—What gin ever came in a sparkling wine bottle? He didn't notice the bubbles?—but the drink tastes delicious, regardless. You can try a 1:1:1 ratio here, but we opt for a bigger pour of sparkling wine.

3 ounces Prosecco

1 ounce Campari

1 ounce sweet vermouth

1 orange slice for garnish

In a large rocks glass filled with ice, combine all the ingredients. Stir gently and briefly. Garnish with a thin half-moon slice of orange.

TIP: If you chill all the ingredients well beforehand, you can serve this drink in a flute without ice, but we prefer it on the rocks.

EVERY COCKTAIL HAS A TWIST

MONTEGRONI

A whole kingdom of bitter Italian liqueurs has some commonality with Campari. We adore the rich, orangey Montenegro in this Negroni variation, with gin and sweet vermouth as strong background players to the amaro's inherent complexity.

1½ ounces Amaro
   Montenegro
1 ounce gin
1 ounce sweet vermouth
1 orange peel for garnish

In a mixing glass, combine all the ingredients. Fill the mixing glass three-quarters full of ice. Stir for 30 seconds and strain into a rocks glass filled with ice. Express a 3–4-inch strip of orange peel, skin side down, over the surface of the drink, run the skin around the rim of the glass to distribute the citrus oils, and add the peel, skin side up, to the cocktail.

DAYTIME NEGRONI

The Negroni isn't a subtle drink. Every element comes on strong. If you like the idea of a Negroni but want something a little lighter, try this version. The juicy Cappelletti and bright, fragrant Lillet give this drink real complexity and a gorgeous red hue atop the calmer base of vodka.

1½ ounces vodka
1 ounce Cappelletti
1 ounce Lillet Blanc
1 orange peel for garnish

In a mixing glass, combine all the ingredients. Fill the mixing glass three-quarters full of ice. Stir for 30 seconds and strain into a chilled coupe. Express a 3–4-inch strip of orange peel, skin side down, over the surface of the drink, run the skin around the rim of the glass to distribute the citrus oils, and add the peel, skin side up, to the cocktail.

SLOE GIN NEGRONI

Making sloe gin—a gin steeped with tart sloe berries (related to plums) and sugar—is a traditional British pastime, the kind of concoction for which your family might have a secret recipe. You also can find great commercial brands, such as Spirit Works Sloe Gin from California. With a sweetness and fruit flavor of its own, sloe gin takes well to cocktails. It works perfectly in a Negroni after you shake up the ratios a little. Upping the Campari for balance is the way to go.

1½ ounces Campari

1 ounce sloe gin

½ ounce sweet vermouth

1 dash grapefruit bitters

1 lemon peel for garnish

In a mixing glass, combine all the ingredients. Fill the mixing glass three-quarters full of ice. Stir for 30 seconds and strain into a rocks glass filled with ice. Express a 3-inch strip of lemon peel, skin side down, over the surface of the drink, run the skin around the rim of the glass to distribute the citrus oils, and add the peel, skin side up, to the cocktail.

BUY THIS BOTTLE

Spirit Works Sloe Gin

NEGRONI BIANCO

You can make a white Negroni in any number of ways that retain the drink's bitter, herbal character while swapping out the crimson Campari. This recipe uses the pale but powerful Luxardo Bitter Bianco with aromatic bianco vermouth and grapefruit bitters.

1½ ounces gin

1 ounce bianco vermouth

1 ounce Luxardo Bitter
  Bianco

2 dashes grapefruit bitters

1 lemon peel for garnish

In a mixing glass, combine all the ingredients. Fill the mixing glass three-quarters full of ice. Stir for 30 seconds and strain into a rocks glass filled with ice. Express a 3-inch strip of lemon peel, skin side down, over the surface of the drink, run the skin around the rim of the glass to distribute the citrus oils, and add the peel, skin side up, to the cocktail.

NIGHT WATCH

Campari's bitter bite integrates seamlessly with cold brew. A small measure of coffee gives this drink a rich, complex backdrop, and shaking the drink gives it a bit of a frothy head. Try it when you need a little caffeine with your **digestivo.**

1 ounce Campari

1 ounce gin

½ ounce sweet vermouth

½ ounce cold brew
  concentrate

1 lemon peel for garnish

In a cocktail shaker, combine all the ingredients. Fill the shaker with ice and seal it. Shake vigorously for 15 seconds and strain into a rocks glass filled with ice. Express a 3-inch strip of lemon peel, skin side down, over the surface of the drink, run the skin around the rim of the glass to distribute the citrus oils, and add the peel, skin side up, to the cocktail.

MIX AND MATCH

As a rule, lighter amari work better with lighter spirits. Aperol can't handle a brawny Scotch, and Cynar will overwhelm vodka. Not every combination will work, but you'll have fun trying.

SPIRIT (1 TO 1½ OUNCES)

Bourbon

brandy (applejack, Cognac, Pisco)

gin

mezcal (Tequila)

rum

Scotch

vodka

+

BITTER LIQUEUR (1 OUNCE)

amari (Lo-Fi Gentian,
   Montenegro, Nonino)

Aperol

Campari

Cappelletti

Cynar

Pimm's

Suze

+

WINE-BASED MODIFIER (1 OUNCE)

Byrrh

Cocchi Americano

Dubonnet

Lillet (Blanc, Rosé)

Port (ruby)

Sherry (Amontillado, oloroso)

vermouth (dry, sweet)

> **TIP:** You can find many excellent sweet vermouths. Simply swapping the vermouth—the richer Carpano Antica Formula for, say, the more bitter Punt e Mes—can yield quite a different drink.

+

GARNISH

grapefruit slice

grapefruit twist

lemon twist

lemon wheel

orange slice

orange twist

CAREY'S FAVORITE MIX AND MATCH

rum + Campari + Sherry + grapefruit twist

JOHN'S FAVORITE MIX AND MATCH

Bourbon + Cynar + vermouth + lemon twist

18.

OLD-FASHIONEDS

HISTORIC · POTENT · ROBUST

Let's make an Old-Fashioned...

A drink considered old-fashioned, even in its heyday, the Old-Fashioned has become a staple at cocktail bars and more casual establishments alike. American whiskey has never been more popular, and the esteem of the Old-Fashioned has risen right along with it.

You don't get the name Old-Fashioned without a whole lot of history. From the early 1800s, people drank the Whiskey Cocktail—not a generic term, but a specific libation of whiskey, water, sugar, and bitters. By the 1880s, bartenders were experimenting more and more with cocktails, and, eschewing newfangled drinks such as the Manhattan, some drinkers preferred their whiskey cocktails the old-fashioned way, asking for an "old-fashioned cocktail" (hence the hyphen). Over time, that phrase shortened to Old-Fashioned.

The Old-Fashioned consists of a spirit, most often whiskey, traditionally bourbon or rye; bitters, typically Angostura but we like orange bitters, too; sweetener; and, critically, a big citrus twist because citrus oils form an essential component of the cocktail. You might have noticed that we didn't mention a cocktail cherry or an orange slice. Neither was part of the traditional recipe. Fruit crept into the cocktail during Prohibition, a style firmly established by midcentury.

In its purest form, the Old-Fashioned beautifully showcases the base spirit, and making a proper one shows off your skills as a bartender: your command of the classics, your attention to detail, and so on. Master it, and you'll go far.

Once you have a handle on the template, there's endless room for experimentation. (You might be tempted to Old-Fashion every spirit you come across, and you should!) In these recipes, you'll play with the base spirit; the sweetener, using honey syrup, maple syrup, cinnamon honey syrup, pecan orgeat; and the many, compelling, distinctive bitters available today. However you make yours, don't forget the twist.

BUY THESE BOTTLES

Use a good American whiskey here, either Bourbon or rye. For the Old-Fashioned, you want spirits with a bit of history: Old Forester Bourbon and Rittenhouse rye.

OUR CLASSIC OLD-FASHIONED

No introduction necessary.

2 ounces Bourbon or rye

½ ounce Simple Syrup
   (page 255)

2 dashes Angostura bitters

1 dash orange bitters

1 orange peel for garnish

1 lemon peel for garnish

In a mixing glass, combine all the ingredients. Fill the mixing glass three-quarters full of ice. Stir for 30 seconds and strain into a rocks glass filled with ice. Express a 3-inch strip of orange peel, skin side down, over the surface of the drink, run the skin around the rim of the glass to distribute the citrus oils, and add the peel, skin side up, to the cocktail. Repeat with a 3–4-inch strip of lemon peel.

TIP: We use simple syrup because it allows the sugar to incorporate fully into the cocktail. You can use a sugar cube, though, if you build the drink in the glass. Here's how: Add 1 sugar cube to the bottom of a rocks glass. Add 1 dash bitters onto the cube and muddle. Add whiskey and ice, stir, and garnish. All the sugar might not dissolve, which will make for a stiffer-tasting drink.

MUDDLED OLD-FASHIONED

Apart from the citrus twist, you don't need fruit for an Old-Fashioned. The "fruit salad" version remains as a relic of Prohibition, when the quality of available alcohol dropped precipitously and needed something to mask it. The style stuck for decades. Though times have changed, it turns out that you can make a pretty tasty fruity Old-Fashioned. Use a 100-proof rye here, such as Rittenhouse. You need a brawny whiskey to counter the sweetness of the fruit. No cocktail cherries here (page 116), you want the bright red ones.

1 orange slice
   (approximately ¼ inch
   thick, 10g), halved

3 maraschino cherries, plus
   1 for garnish

2 sugar cubes

2 dashes Angostura bitters

2 ounces rye

In a large rocks glass, layer a half-moon slice of orange, the maraschino cherries, and sugar cubes, add the bitters and muddle thoroughly until the sugar breaks up and dissolves in the fruit juice and bitters. Add the rye, fill the glass with ice, then stir to incorporate fully, about 30 seconds. Garnish with another half-moon slice of orange and another maraschino cherry.

LAST CALL

You have to use old-fashioned bitters in an Old-Fashioned, right? We like Fee Brothers Old Fashioned Aromatic Bitters because it goes bold on the cinnamon and spice, anchoring the rye and maple of this cocktail. It's a novel combination of familiar flavors, one of those drinks that's really more than the sum of its parts.

2 ounces rye

½ ounce maple syrup

1 dash old-fashioned bitters

1 orange peel for garnish

1 lemon peel for garnish

In a mixing glass, combine all the ingredients. Fill the mixing glass three-quarters full of ice. Stir for 30 seconds and strain into a rocks glass filled with ice. Express a 3–4-inch strip of orange peel, skin side down, over the surface of the drink, run the skin around the rim of the glass to distribute the citrus oils, and add the peel, skin side up, to the cocktail. Repeat with a 3-inch strip of lemon peel.

FIRESIDE

Every dark spirit has a home in the Old-Fashioned. A good dark rum has all the barrel-aged character of a fine whiskey. Here, you'll balance rum's natural sweetness with dry, powerfully flavored allspice dram. This properly stiff drink has all the comforting warm-spice flavors perfect for winter. Repeat with a 3-inch strip of lemon peel.

2 ounces dark rum

¼ ounce allspice dram

½ ounce Raw Sugar Syrup
   (page 256)

1 dash Angostura bitters

1 orange peel for garnish

In a mixing glass, combine all the ingredients. Fill the mixing glass three-quarters full of ice. Stir for 30 seconds and strain into a rocks glass filled with ice. Express a 3–4-inch strip of orange peel, skin side down, over the surface of the drink, run the skin around the rim of the glass to distribute the citrus oils, and add the peel, skin side up, to the cocktail.

PECAN OLD-FASHIONED

The oaky-vanilla warmth of a good Bourbon perfectly matches nutty flavors. Here a pecan orgeat brings its own toasty flavors front and center. Angostura bitters balance the nuttiness in this one part festive dessert, one part serious cocktail.

2 ounces Bourbon

1 ounce Pecan Orgeat
   (page 258)

1 dash Angostura bitters

1 orange peel for garnish

Freshly grated nutmeg for
   garnish

In a mixing glass, combine all the ingredients. Fill the mixing glass three-quarters full of ice. Stir for 30 seconds and strain into a rocks glass filled with ice. Express a 3–4-inch strip of orange peel, skin side down, over the surface of the drink, run the skin around the rim of the glass to distribute the citrus oils, and add the peel, skin side up, to the cocktail. Garnish with the nutmeg.

OPENING BID

Let's think beyond American whiskey. Here, blended Scotch serves as the base for a cascade of flavor: rich honey, floral St-Germain, and anise-tinged Peychaud's bitters. It tastes a little mysterious, a lot delicious.

2 ounces blended Scotch
   whisky

½ ounce St-Germain
   elderflower liqueur

½ ounce Honey Syrup
   (page 255)

1 dash Peychaud's bitters

1 round grapefruit peel for
   garnish

1 lemon peel for garnish

In a mixing glass, combine all the ingredients. Fill the mixing glass three-quarters full of ice. Stir for 30 seconds and strain into a rocks glass filled with ice. Express a 1-inch round of grapefruit peel, skin side down, over the surface of the drink, run the skin around the rim of the glass to distribute the citrus oils, and add the peel, skin side up, to the cocktail. Repeat with a 3-inch strip of lemon peel.

AÑEJO OLD-FASHIONED

This popular drink from our book Be Your Own Bartender *perfectly illustrates the versatility of the Old-Fashioned, which can stretch far beyond whiskey. Rich Tequila añejo ("aged") stars in this cocktail, with Angostura and chocolate bitters to complement.*

2 ounces Tequila añejo

¼ ounce Dark Agave Syrup (page 256)

1 dash orange bitters

1 dash Fee Brothers Aztec Chocolate Bitters

1 round grapefruit peel for garnish

1 orange peel for garnish

In a mixing glass, combine all the ingredients. Fill the mixing glass three-quarters full of ice. Stir for 30 seconds and strain into a rocks glass filled with ice. Express a 1-inch round of grapefruit peel, skin side down, over the surface of the drink, then discard. Express a 3–4-inch strip of orange peel, skin side down, over the surface of the drink, run the skin around the rim of the glass to distribute the citrus oils, and add the peel, skin side up, to the cocktail.

CORDUROY

In virtually any recipe that calls for whiskey, you can use apple brandy. For this stiff and satisfying cocktail, use Laird's Straight Apple Brandy Bottled in Bond at 100 proof. Cinnamon and honey make natural bedfellows for pure autumn flavor.

2 ounces apple brandy

½ ounce Cinnamon Honey Syrup (page 256)

1 dash Angostura bitters

1 lemon peel for garnish

In a mixing glass, combine all the ingredients. Fill the mixing glass three-quarters full of ice. Stir for 30 seconds and strain into a rocks glass filled with ice. Express a 3-inch strip of lemon peel, skin side down, over the surface of the drink, run the skin around the rim of the glass to distribute the citrus oils, and add the peel, skin side up, to the cocktail.

AN OLD-FASHIONED PARTY

MAKES 6 DRINKS

It's not an obvious candidate for a pitcher drink, but the Old-Fashioned has become popular enough that you might want to prebatch a round or two for poker nights, bachelor/ette parties, a particularly festive Thanksgiving, or other great occasions. Again, when batching any stirred drink, you need to include a little water, which replicates the ice melt from stirring. From there, just pour over ice and garnish.

12 ounces rye or Bourbon

6 ounces water

3 ounces Simple Syrup (page 255)

6 dashes Angostura bitters

6 dashes orange bitters

6 orange peels for garnish

6 lemon peels for garnish

In a quart container or 1 liter bottle, combine all the ingredients. Store in the freezer until ready to serve. To serve, divide the mixture equally among six rocks glasses filled with ice, about 3½ ounces per glass. For each drink, express a 3- to 4-inch strip of orange peel, skin side down, over the surface of each drink, run the skin around the rim of the glass to distribute the citrus oils, and add the peel, skin side up, to the cocktail. Repeat with a 3-inch strip of lemon peel.

MIX AND MATCH

Stir up a newfangled Old-Fashioned. You *could* use vodka, but why? Choose a dark spirit or something with a little age. You probably already have a bottle of Angostura bitters at home, so start there and then explore. For the sweetener, simple syrup will do, but so will just about anything sweet. Using cocktail syrups introduces additional layers of flavor. The final touch, a citrus garnish imparts a bright burst of flavor. Lime isn't common, but don't let that stop you from experimenting with it.

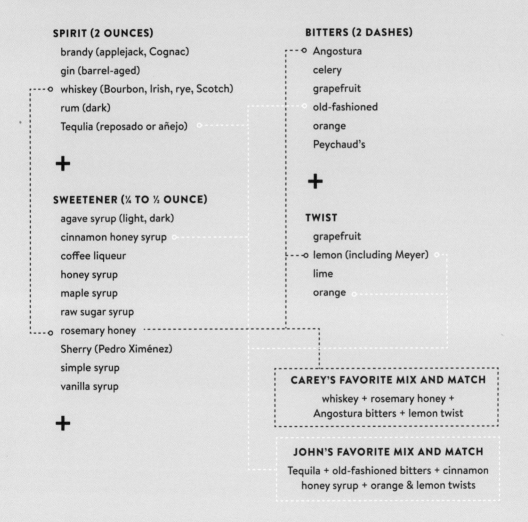

SPIRIT (2 OUNCES)
brandy (applejack, Cognac)
gin (barrel-aged)
whiskey (Bourbon, Irish, rye, Scotch)
rum (dark)
Tequlia (reposado or añejo)

+

SWEETENER (¼ TO ½ OUNCE)
agave syrup (light, dark)
cinnamon honey syrup
coffee liqueur
honey syrup
maple syrup
raw sugar syrup
rosemary honey
Sherry (Pedro Ximénez)
simple syrup
vanilla syrup

+

BITTERS (2 DASHES)
Angostura
celery
grapefruit
old-fashioned
orange
Peychaud's

+

TWIST
grapefruit
lemon (including Meyer)
lime
orange

CAREY'S FAVORITE MIX AND MATCH
whiskey + rosemary honey +
Angostura bitters + lemon twist

JOHN'S FAVORITE MIX AND MATCH
Tequila + old-fashioned bitters + cinnamon
honey syrup + orange & lemon twists

19.

PALOMAS

TANGY · VIBRANT · INVIGORATING

I'd like a Paloma . . .

When you think of a Tequila cocktail, you picture the Margarita, right? We all do. But you should get to know another Tequila drink: the fresh, juicy Paloma.

In its traditional form, the Paloma is just a highball consisting of Tequila blanco with grapefruit soda (traditionally Squirt), a squeeze of lime, and a salted rim or a pinch of salt. Origin stories differ, but Squirt, created in Arizona in 1938, made its way to Mexico in 1955. Its union with Tequila likely soon followed.

The standard booze-and-soda Paloma represents the kind of informal, no-recipe-required drink ideal for a party.

Set the bottles out with some ice, limes, and salt, and let everyone have at it. But we bartenders love to dress things up. A Paloma with fresh grapefruit juice has its own juicy appeal, and from there, the riffs are endless. Add a little heat, a splash of Aperol, or use smoky mezcal. Make an elegant cocktail version with pamplemousse liqueur, or skip the Tequila altogether for Bourbon. You can have fun with that salt rim, too.

QUICK PALOMA

We tried half a dozen grapefruit sodas for this recipe, and Squirt won by a mile with exactly the right balance of tart and sweet to stand up to a healthy pour of Tequila. Salting the rim is always an option, but for this drink we prefer a small pinch of salt in the glass.

4 ounces Squirt

1½ ounces Tequila blanco

1 pinch kosher salt

1 lime wedge for garnish

In a Collins glass filled with ice, combine all the ingredients. Stir gently and briefly. Squeeze a lime wedge into the glass and drop it in.

JUICY PALOMA

Prefer real juice to sweet soda? This recipe makes use of ruby red grapefruit, a bit of lime, and agave to balance the citrus. Bright, fun, and easy drinking.

1½ ounces Tequila blanco

2 ounces ruby red grapefruit juice

½ ounce lime juice

½ ounce Light Agave Syrup (page 255)

2 ounces club soda

1 ruby red grapefruit slice for garnish

In a cocktail shaker, combine all the ingredients except the club soda. Fill the shaker with ice and seal it. Shake vigorously for 15 seconds and strain into a Collins glass filled with ice. Top with the club soda and stir gently and briefly. Garnish with a thin half-moon slice of grapefruit.

EVERY COCKTAIL HAS A TWIST

DERBY PALOMA

The Paloma contains Tequila—fine. But grapefruit and lime pair well with many spirits, Bourbon among them. Halfway between the Bourbon-grapefruit sour Brown Derby and a Paloma proper, it tastes just as refreshing as the original but with a little more depth. Don't skip the salt.

1½ ounces Bourbon

1 ounce grapefruit juice

¾ ounce Light Agave Syrup (page 255)

½ ounce lime juice

1 pinch kosher salt

2 ounces club soda

1 grapefruit slice for garnish

In a cocktail shaker, combine all the ingredients except the club soda. Fill the shaker with ice and seal it. Shake vigorously for 15 seconds and strain into a Collins glass filled with ice. Top with the club soda and stir gently and briefly. Garnish with a thin half-moon slice of grapefruit.

SPICY PALOMA

The Spicy Margarita has become a staple in its own right, so why not spice up the Paloma, too? Infusing the pepper into the Tequila gives you more control over the heat in the finished drink. From there, just add Squirt.

1½ ounces Serrano-Infused Tequila (page 261)

4 ounces Squirt

1 lime wedge for garnish

In a Collins glass filled with ice, combine the Tequila and Squirt. Stir gently and briefly. Squeeze the lime wedge into the glass and drop it in.

BATCH IT

For 6 drinks, combine 9 ounces of infused Tequila with 24 ounces (two cans) of Squirt in a pitcher with ice. Garnish with lime wedges.

MAI TAI PALOMA

Orgeat imparts a nutty complexity to this drink, taking it halfway to tiki territory. If you don't want to make your own, look for the Small Hand Foods brand. An elaborate garnish makes sense here.

1½ ounces Tequila blanco

½ ounce pamplemousse
   liqueur

½ ounce grapefruit juice

½ ounce lime juice

½ ounce Orgeat (page 258)

1½ ounces club soda

1 grapefruit slice for garnish

1 pineapple slice for garnish
   (optional)

In a cocktail shaker, combine all the ingredients except the club soda. Fill the shaker with ice and seal it. Shake vigorously for 15 seconds and strain into a Collins glass filled with ice. Top with the club soda and stir gently and briefly. Have fun with the garnish: a thin half-moon slice of grapefruit and, if you like, a thin triangle of pineapple. Serve with a cocktail umbrella.

OUTER SUNSET

Grapefruit has a natural affinity for other bitter flavors. Here, earthy, vegetal Cynar adds a bitter sophistication to a usually lighthearted drink. The final touch? Rim the glass not just with salt but with a grapefruit-zested salt that adds another dimension of flavor.

Grapefruit Salt (page 261)
   to rim

1½ ounces Tequila blanco

1 ounce grapefruit juice

½ ounce Cynar

¼ ounce lime juice

¼ ounce Light Agave Syrup
   (page 255)

2 ounces club soda

Rim a Collins glass with the grapefruit salt. Set aside the prepared glass. In a cocktail shaker, combine all the ingredients except the club soda. Fill the shaker with ice and seal it. Shake vigorously for 15 seconds and strain into a Collins glass filled with ice. Top with the club soda and stir gently and briefly.

PHOENIX RISING

Like the Paloma, El Diablo is an underappreciated Tequila classic, which incorporates ginger beer and Cassis. This drink brings the two ideas together. Ginger and Cassis happen to pair nicely with grapefruit juice and a bit of smoky mezcal for good measure. Layered flavors of fruit, ginger, and spirit make this drink complex but supremely enjoyable.

1 ounce Tequila reposado

1 ounce ruby red grapefruit
   juice

½ ounce mezcal

½ ounce lime juice

½ ounce crème de Cassis

¼ ounce Light Agave Syrup
   (page 255)

2 ounces ginger beer

1 grapefruit slice for garnish

1 cocktail cherry for garnish

In a cocktail shaker, combine all the ingredients except the ginger beer. Fill the shaker with ice and seal it. Shake vigorously for 15 seconds and strain into a Collins glass filled with ice. Top with the ginger beer and stir gently and briefly. Garnish with a thin half-moon slice of grapefruit and a cocktail cherry.

PAMPLEOMA

If you like the flavors of the Paloma but prefer something more potent, rather than tall and sparkling, give this version a try. Here you'll swap the grapefruit juice for grapefruit liqueur. Sleek and balanced, it tastes even better with a salt rim accented with aromatic lime zest.

Lime Salt (page 261) to rim

2 ounces Tequila blanco

1 ounce pamplemousse
   liqueur

½ ounce lime juice

½ ounce Light Agave Syrup
   (page 255)

1 dash grapefruit bitters

Rim a rocks glass with lime salt. Set aside the prepared glass. In a cocktail shaker, combine all the ingredients. Fill the shaker with ice and seal it. Shake vigorously for 15 seconds and strain into the prepared glass filled with ice.

PALOMA SPRITZ

Every Paloma can work as a fun, sunny day drink, and this version even more so, with assists from Aperol and herbaceous rosemary honey. Rather than Squirt, use San Pellegrino Pompelmo soda, which has the appealing bitterness of white grapefruit.

Grapefruit Salt (page 261) to rim

1½ ounces Tequila blanco

½ ounce Aperol

½ ounce grapefruit juice

¼ ounce lime juice

¼ ounce Rosemary Honey (page 256)

2 ounces San Pellegrino Pompelmo soda

1 lime wedge for garnish

1 rosemary sprig for garnish

Rim a wine glass with the grapefruit salt. Set aside the prepared glass. In a cocktail shaker, combine all the ingredients except the soda. Fill the shaker with ice and seal it. Shake vigorously for 15 seconds and strain into the prepared glass filled with ice. Top with the soda, squeeze a lime wedge into the glass, and stir gently and briefly. Drop in the squeezed lime wedge. Clap a rosemary sprig between your palms and add it to the drink.

20.

PIMM'S CUPS

LIQUID GARDEN PARTY

Let's make a Pimm's Cup . . .

Most spirits and liqueurs have plenty of familiar uses. You'll come across gin in the Martini, Tom Collins, Negroni—you name it. But Pimm's is something of an anomaly. You drink it in a Pimm's Cup . . . and that's about it, which is a shame because it tastes delicious. Warming and complex, its balanced sweetness and gentle bitterness shine in cocktails, and the 25% ABV makes it boozy enough to anchor a drink but mellow enough to keep it light and easygoing.

In its very simplest form, the Pimm's Cup contains Pimm's No. 1 liqueur—an English gin-based liqueur dating to the nineteenth century—mixed with lemonade or ginger ale and served tall. It often features elaborate garnishes: cucumber, mint, strawberry, or all of the above. More festive Pimm's Cups generally include those fruits and herbs within the drinks themselves.

Like the Mint Julep, it's an occasion-specific drink, rather than something to order off-menu at a bar, in America anyway. The quintessential Mint Julep goes with the Kentucky Derby, while the quintessential Pimm's Cup enlivens an English garden party. They both take a bit of preparation but, when served, become absolute showstoppers.

We'll take you through the whole world of Pimm's Cups, from a two-ingredient highball easy enough for a Tuesday night, through elaborate cocktail versions, to outside-the-box drinks that swap out the Pimm's entirely. Cheers!

BASIC PIMM'S CUP

Whether you're already a fan or haven't had the opportunity to try one, it's worth sipping the drink in its simplest form before raiding the produce drawer. Make this recipe—it's not much more complicated than pouring a beer—for a low-effort evening.

2 ounces Pimm's No. 1

4 ounces ginger ale or
   sparkling lemonade

1 cucumber slice for garnish

In a Collins glass filled with ice, combine the Pimm's No. 1 and ginger ale. Stir gently and briefly. Garnish with a thin cucumber slice nestled between the ice and the glass.

Why No. 1?

In 19th-century London, James Pimm, the proprietor of an oyster bar, devised the gin-based concoction that bears his name as a digestive aid. With popularity booming, he bottled it, then sold it beyond his bar. Further cups followed:

No. 2 Scotch

No. 3 brandy

No. 4 dark rum

No. 5 rye

No. 6 vodka

No. 7 Tequila

Diageo still sells a very limited amount of No. 3 and No. 6 in the United Kingdom, but No. 1 has stood the test of time, thanks to its signature drink.

FANCY DRESS PIMM'S

The basic Pimm's Cup tastes undeniably delicious, but to understand its appeal as a party drink, you have to break out the muddler and get ready to garnish. There's a lot of produce in this fancy version, but we promise, it's worth it. Pimm's comes alive in a cocktail that tastes fruity but not too sweet, made refreshing with strawberry, cucumber, and ginger. With that abundance of fresh ingredients, we add a little straight gin to stiffen it and ginger beer to amplify the flavor.

1 piece peeled ginger (approximately 1 inch long, ½ inch thick, 5g), quartered

1 cucumber slice (approximately ½ inch thick, 20g), plus 1 for garnish

1 medium strawberry, hulled and halved

1 ounce gin

1 ounce Pimm's No. 1

¼ ounce lemon juice

¼ ounce Simple Syrup (page 255)

3 leaves mint, torn in half just before adding to shaker

2 ounces ginger beer

1 lemon wheel for garnish

1 sprig mint for garnish

In the bottom of a cocktail shaker, add the ginger and muddle firmly until well smashed. Add the cucumber slice and half the strawberry and muddle again. Add the remaining ingredients except the ginger beer. Fill the shaker with ice and seal it. Shake vigorously for 15 seconds and double strain into a Collins glass filled with ice. Top with the ginger beer and stir gently and briefly. Garnish with abandon: a slice of cucumber, a lemon wheel, and the remaining half of the strawberry. Lightly tap a mint sprig against your hand to release the aromatic oils before adding it to the glass.

TIP: If you like, you can swap the Pimm's for vodka or white rum.

PITCHER PIMM'S

MAKES 6 DRINKS

Muddled drinks aren't the easiest to make for a party, but after much R&D, we've found the best way to make a pitcher of Pimm's Cup. Whiz it all up in a blender, strain into a pitcher, and add club soda. You usually use the blender for frozen drinks, but here it makes quick work of the many ingredients, leaving you with a vibrant cocktail. In the fridge, it will last about 24 hours without any decline in quality, but don't let it go longer than that.

~~~~~~

8 ounces Pimm's No. 1

6 ounces gin

4 ounces Simple Syrup
   (page 255)

2½ ounces lemon juice

1 cucumber segment
   (3 inches long, 120g),
   peeled and roughly
   chopped (see Note), plus
   6 slices for garnish

1 piece peeled ginger
   (approximately 1 inch
   long, 1 inch thick, 10g),
   roughly chopped

18 leaves mint

3 large strawberries
   (approximately 48g),
   hulled, plus 3 more,
   halved, for garnish

12 ounces club soda

6 lemon wheels for garnish

6 sprigs mint for garnish

In a blender, combine all the ingredients except the club soda. Blend until smooth. Strain through a fine-mesh strainer into a pitcher and discard the solids. Add ice and the club soda. To serve, divide equally among six Collins glasses filled with ice and garnish away: 6 thin bias-cut slices of cucumber, 6 lemon wheels, and 6 strawberry halves. Lightly tap the mint sprigs against your hand to release their aromatic oils before adding to the glasses.

NOTE: It's another step, but make sure to peel the cucumber before you add it to the blender. That will keep the drink's color pleasantly reddish rather than murky brown.

PIMM'S SHANDY

Above all, a Pimm's Cup should taste refreshing and be easy drinking. A shandy, another classic drink in this model, consists of beer and lemonade. So let's combine the two. Using a lighter beer, such as a Pilsner or blonde ale, keeps it bright and crisp. Best consumed poolside.

1½ ounces Pimm's No. 1

¼ ounce lemon juice

¼ ounce Simple Syrup
(page 255)

10 leaves mint, torn in half
just before added to
shaker

2 ounces Pilsner or blonde
ale

2 or 3 large sprigs mint for
garnish

1 lemon wheel for garnish

In a cocktail shaker, combine all the ingredients except the beer. Fill the shaker with ice and seal it. Shake vigorously for 15 seconds and double strain into a tall glass filled with ice. Top with the beer and stir gently and briefly. Lightly tap the mint sprigs against your hand to release their aromatic oils before adding them to the drink. Also garnish with a lemon wheel.

GREEN PIMM'S

If you love a good green juice at a smoothie shop or on a brunch menu, this is the Pimm's for you. It takes the friendly cucumber garnish of the classic Pimm's Cup and amplifies it with celery and basil. The smallest pinch of salt adds the finishing touch. The drink won't taste salty in the slightest; the salt brings the vegetal elements together. Ginger beer contributes just a little more spice.

2 celery pieces (2 inches long, 30g), plus 1 thin spear for garnish

1 cucumber slice (approximately ½ inch thick, 20g), plus 1 long, thin slice for garnish

3 basil leaves, torn in half just before added to shaker, plus 1 sprig for garnish

1½ ounces Pimm's No. 1

¼ ounce lemon juice

¼ ounce Simple Syrup (page 255)

1 pinch salt

1½ ounces ginger beer

In the bottom of a cocktail shaker, add the celery and cucumber and muddle until the pieces break up, then add the basil and muddle again lightly. Add the remaining ingredients except the ginger beer. Fill the shaker with ice and seal it. Shake vigorously for 15 seconds and double strain into a Collins glass filled with ice. Top with the ginger beer and stir gently and briefly. Garnish with the cucumber slice and celery spear. Lightly tap the basil sprig against your hand to release the aromatic oils before adding it to the drink.

MONTENEGRO CUP

At heart, the Pimm's Cup functions as a light, low-proof highball with an elaborate garnish. But why should Pimm's alone receive that treatment? For this version, reach for the warm and citrusy Amaro Montenegro. Like Pimm's, its complexity shines in a bright, vibrant highball with plenty of summery fruits and herbs.

1 cucumber slice (approximately ½ inch thick, 20g), plus 1 slice for garnish

1 medium strawberry, hulled and halved

1½ ounces Amaro Montenegro

¼ ounce lemon juice

¼ ounce Simple Syrup (page 255)

10 leaves mint, plus 1 sprig to garnish

3 ounces ginger ale

1 orange slice for garnish

In the bottom of a cocktail shaker, add the cucumber and muddle it hard, then add half the strawberry and muddle again lightly. Add the remaining ingredients except the ginger ale. Fill the shaker with ice and seal it. Shake vigorously for 15 seconds and double strain into a Collins glass filled with ice. Top with the ginger ale and stir gently and briefly. Garnish with a half-moon slice of orange, a half-moon slice of cucumber, and the other strawberry half. Lightly tap a mint sprig against your hand to release the aromatic oils before adding to the glass.

FROZEN PIMM'S

MAKES 4 DRINKS

A classic day drink, Pimm's is ideal for hot afternoons on the porch or in the garden. The only way to make it more refreshing? Ice, baby, and blending the classic garnishes right into the drink. It's everything a strawberry Daiquirí wishes it was.

6 ounces Pimm's No. 1

2 ounces Simple Syrup
(page 255)

1 ounce lemon juice

4 cucumber slices
(approximately ¼ inch
thick, 80g), plus 4 slices
for garnish

4 medium strawberries
(approximately 50g),
hulled, plus 2 for garnish

1 piece peeled ginger
(approximately ½ inch
long, ¼ inch thick, 2g)

12 leaves mint, plus 4 sprigs
for garnish

In a blender, combine all the ingredients and add 4 cups of ice. Blend until smooth. Divide equally among four Collins glasses and garnish with the cucumber slices and half-strawberries. Lightly tap the mint sprigs against your hand to release their aromatic oils before adding to the glasses. Serve with straws.

21.

SANGRIAS

WINE + BOOZE = PARTY!

I'd like some Sangria . . .

Ah, sangria. It can be a vibrant, nuanced punch that's a joy to sip—or it can taste like a cloying mess, all syrupy wine and mushy fruit. At heart, sangria is as versatile as it is fun, an opportunity to bring together wine, fruit, and spirits to delicious effect.

First, let's dispense with the ghosts of sangrias past so we can get to the good stuff. The sangrias you've had before, at restaurants in particular, may not have impressed you. They might have contained bottom-shelf wine ($5 Merlot) or, worse, open bottles of red from the night before. Added sugar sometimes masks the flavor of subpar wine or cheap liquor, and the combination of sugar, wine, and booze can leave you with a nasty headache. Despite its wine base, Sangria can run deceptively strong, and a stronger drink isn't always better.

But sangria is one of our favorite drinks to play with. You can use red wine, white wine, even bubbles. You can use fresh fruit, grilled fruit, Bourbon-soaked fruit—endless possibilities. Since you're making a whole batch at once, it's worth taking time to prep. When guests arrive, just pour and enjoy. If you want a single-serve, two-second sangria hack with no prep whatsoever, we've got a trick for that, too.

SANGRIA ESPAÑOLA

MAKES 4 TO 6 DRINKS

Good sangria has nuance and an intriguing balance of flavors that you can't always pinpoint but that entice you to take another sip. For this rich red sangria, you'll use two unorthodox ingredients: herbal gin and sweet vermouth. Together, they contribute a depth of flavor that belies the recipe's simplicity. You also will use one orange in two ways: the peel for a citrus syrup known as oleo saccharum (page 260) and the fruit itself to soak in the sangria.

If you can, go all Spanish here with Gin Mare, a juicy red vermouth such as Yzaguirre Rojo Reserva, and a Tempranillo wine such as la Nevera Tinto Rioja (a first-class boxed wine and an insane value).

1 orange, peeled (peels reserved for the oleo saccharum) and segmented (approximately 150g), plus 4 thin slices for garnish (optional)

12½ ounces (½ bottle) red wine

1 cup sweet vermouth

2 ounces gin

2 ounces Orange Oleo Saccharum (page 260)

Cut each orange segment into thirds. In a sealable container, combine all the ingredients except the oleo saccharum, and refrigerate overnight. Make the oleo saccharum at the same time and allow to rest overnight. Before serving, stir the oleo saccharum into the chilled sangria. Serve in rocks glasses filled with ice, along with the wine-soaked orange pieces, and, if you like, additional orange slices for color.

EVERY COCKTAIL HAS A TWIST

GRILLED PINEAPPLE SANGRIA

MAKES 4 TO 6 DRINKS

It's fresh, juicy, nuanced, and easy drinking. This sangria is a winner! It stars grilled pineapple, which picks up an appealing caramelized flavor from the heat. Joining it are a light white wine, coconut water, and the South American brandy Pisco. A crowd pleaser for all the right reasons. We like using a Spanish white here, such as Macabeo (Viura), but anything light-bodied and brightly acidic will work.

12½ ounces (½ bottle) light white wine

1 cup coconut water

4 ounces Pisco

2 ounces Raw Sugar Syrup (page 256)

1 ounce lemon juice

1 ounce lime juice

4 Grilled Pineapple rounds (approximately 1 inch thick, 350g, page 159), cut into chunks

In a sealable container, combine all the ingredients and refrigerate overnight. Pour into rocks glasses filled with ice. Garnish with the soaked pineapple chunks.

ROSÉ ALL DAY

MAKES 4 TO 6 DRINKS

Sparkling sangria? Oh, yeah! You don't add the sparkling wine in advance, of course, which would kill all the bubbles. Instead, let the other elements steep overnight to combine, then add the bubbles just before serving. It's the most elegant brunch drink you ever did see, with no juicing, muddling, or blending required.

4 ounces Lillet Blanc

2 ounces Cognac

1 ounce St-Germain
   elderflower liqueur

½ cup raspberries
   (approximately 80g)

12½ ounces (½ bottle)
   sparkling rosé, rosado,
   or rosato, well chilled

In a sealable container, combine the Lillet, Cognac, St-Germain, and raspberries and refrigerate overnight. To serve, pour the mixture into a large pitcher. Top with the sparkling wine and stir gently and briefly. Pour into rocks glasses filled with ice and garnish with the soaked raspberries.

TIP: Make this recipe in a *slim* pitcher, and the bubbles will buoy the raspberries up and down like the world's tastiest lava lamp.

SANGRIA BLANCA

MAKES 4 TO 6 DRINKS

Red sangrias take well to warm spice and lots of fruit. White sangrias taste brighter, a little more tart and lively. Here, Tequila and lime lend their unmistakable energy, while white wine and dry, aromatic white Port form the base. Use a fresh, juicy white, such as Vinho Verde or Macabeo (Viura)—no big Chardonnays here. You also don't want the apple to steep overnight because it'll become mushy. Add the apple 1 or 2 hours before serving, long enough to release flavor but not fall apart.

12½ ounces (½ bottle) white
   wine

1 cup white Port

4 ounces Tequila blanco

2 ounces lime juice

4 ounces Light Agave Syrup
   (page 255)

1 green apple

In a sealable container, combine all the ingredients, except the apple, and refrigerate overnight or until chilled. About 1–2 hours before serving, dice the green apple and add it to the container. Pour into rocks glasses filled with ice, adding some of the soaked apple pieces in each glass.

EVERY COCKTAIL HAS A TWIST

PEACH BOURBON SANGRIA

MAKES 6 DRINKS

This southern sangria teems with the flavors of summer. Rather than letting the peaches soak in the wine, infuse them directly into the whiskey. Once you have your peach Bourbon ready to go, pour everything into a pitcher and serve.

12½ ounces (¼ bottle)
   red wine
6 ounces Peach-Infused
   Bourbon (page 261)
1 cup 100% tart cherry juice
3 ounces Honey Syrup
   (page 255)
2 ounces lemon juice
⅛ teaspoon vanilla extract
6 ounces club soda
6 cherries for garnish
6 peach slices for garnish

To serve immediately, in a pitcher, combine the wine, Bourbon, cherry juice, honey syrup, lemon juice, and vanilla extract. To prebatch, in a sealable container, combine the same ingredients and refrigerate overnight. To serve, pour 4 ounces of sangria in each rocks glass and top with 1 ounce club soda. Give a quick, gentle stir and garnish each glass with a fresh cherry and a peach slice.

NOTE: Use 100% tart cherry juice. The ingredients list on the label should contain only cherries and water (no apple or grape).

SANGRIA AHORITA

Should we have taken the time to develop sophisticated Sangria recipes and then share a hack to skip half those steps? Eh, why not. San Pellegrino's juicy sodas are a great cocktail shortcut. Combine their orange-pomegranate soda with some wine and rum and you've got a convincing sangria facsimile. Drink responsibly.

2 ounces red wine

2 ounces San Pellegrino
   Melograno e Arancia
   soda

½ ounce dark rum

1 orange wedge for garnish

Berries of choice for garnish
   (optional)

In a rocks glass or wine glass filled with ice, combine all the ingredients. Squeeze an orange wedge into the glass and drop it in. If the spirit moves you, throw some berries in there, too.

Sangria Española

Rosé All Day

Grilled Pineapple Sangria

Sangria Española

Rosé All Day

Grilled Pineapple
Sangria

22.

SAZERACS

POTENT · BROODING · ENIGMATIC

Let's make a Sazerac that's. . .

Not for novices, the Sazerac. Stiff and uncompromising, it's a *drinker's* drink, one that requires commitment. You don't toss a Sazerac back without thinking. It's also a cerebral drink, the kind that rewards contemplation.

The official cocktail of New Orleans—a city with no shortage of drinks it can claim as its own—the Sazerac was created in the late 1800s at Sazerac House. A classic whiskey cocktail, like the Old-Fashioned and Manhattan, the Sazerac contains rye whiskey, Peychaud's bitters, and absinthe. But it has a few quirks all its own. You drink it from a rocks glass *without* ice. It's boozy as all get-out, and the absinthe rinse is essential. When made properly, the absinthe and anise notes of Peychaud's bitters nicely balance the whiskey. All are bold elements; no wallflowers here.

It's easy to riff on the Margarita or Tom Collins; the Sazerac, perhaps less so. So what do the variations look like? These cocktails all share the same basic presentation: served in a chilled rocks glass, no ice; a stiff spirit backbone; and some hint of the defining anise flavor. Cocktail geeks, take note. These are some of the most nuanced, complex drinks produced from the recipes in this book.

CHILL THAT GLASS

There's no ice in this drink, so you must chill the glass beforehand. Simply chill your glass by stashing it in the freezer or filling it with ice water while you prepare the drink. You want the glass as cold as possible for serving.

OUR CLASSIC SAZERAC

You need Peychaud's bitters for the Sazerac, but we like to sneak Angostura in there, too, for added depth and character. This recipe uses more than the usual amount because, after making many a Sazerac, we love the power of Peychaud's and Angostura together. Give this drink a good long stir for the ice melt to dilute the whiskey and bitters.

For many years, absinthe was illegal in America. Herbsaint, a similar New Orleans–made liqueur, served as a substitute. Now that absinthe has become widely available again, it's our preferred rinse.

2 ounces rye whiskey

¼ ounce Simple Syrup (page 255)

5 dashes Peychaud's bitters

3 dashes Angostura bitters

¼ ounce absinthe for rinsing

1 lemon peel for garnish

Chill a rocks glass in advance. In a mixing glass, combine all the ingredients except the absinthe and fill the mixing glass three-quarters full of ice. Rinse the chilled rocks glass with the absinthe. Stir the mixing glass for 30 seconds and strain into the prepared rocks glass. Express a 1-inch round of lemon peel, skin side down, over the surface of the drink, run the skin around the rim of the glass to distribute the citrus oils, then discard.

RINSING

In a cocktail, certain spirits or liqueurs can dominate everything around them. So how to incorporate that flavor into a drink without it taking over? Consider a rinse. "Rinsing" is exactly what it sounds like: coating the interior of a glass with a liquid. In doing so, you add an element that stands apart from the rest of the drink, neither overwhelming nor muddying the flavors in the cocktail itself.

To rinse, pour about ¼ ounce of your liqueur or spirit into the bottom of a coupe or rocks glass. Gently swirl the liquid around the glass to coat it fully, then pour out the excess liquid so it doesn't pool at the bottom. Alternately, you can use an atomizer spray bottle to spritz a mist of the liqueur or spirit around the inside of the glass. Prepare your cocktail and strain it into the prepared glass.

FORGE ET FILS

The documentation surrounding the Sazerac's invention is thin, but one historian holds that Cognac served as its original base. It switched to rye by the end of the 1800s, when the phylloxera epidemic (vine lice) ravaged French vineyards, drastically reducing the availability of Cognac, a grape brandy. Regardless of whether it's the original, this drink tastes mighty nice with Cognac—smooth, refined, and just as spirited as whiskey.

2 ounces Cognac

¼ ounce Simple Syrup (page 255)

3 dashes Peychaud's bitters

1 dashes Angostura bitters

¼ ounce absinthe for rinsing

1 lemon peel for garnish

Chill a rocks glass in advance. In a mixing glass, combine all the ingredients except the absinthe and fill the mixing glass three-quarters full of ice. Rinse the chilled rocks glass with the absinthe. Stir the mixing glass for 30 seconds and strain into the prepared rocks glass. Express a 1-inch round of lemon peel, skin side down, over the surface of the drink, run the skin around the rim of the glass to distribute the citrus oils, then discard.

CARONDELET STREET

The traditional Sazerac goes bold on flavor and ABV. This version brings the proof down a bit—splitting Cognac with Lillet Rosé, also grape-based—while keeping the drink's essential heft and balance of flavor. A Sherry rinse adds an elusive complexity with nowhere near as much alcohol as absinthe.

1 ounce Cognac

1 ounce Lillet Rosé

¼ ounce Simple Syrup (page 255)

3 dashes Peychaud's bitters

¼ ounce Amontillado Sherry for rinsing

1 lemon peel for garnish

Chill a rocks glass in advance. In a mixing glass, combine all the ingredients except the Sherry and fill the mixing glass three-quarters full of ice. Rinse the chilled rocks glass with the Sherry. Stir the mixing glass for 30 seconds and strain into the prepared rocks glass. Express a 1-inch round of lemon peel, skin side down, over the surface of the drink, run the skin around the rim of the glass to distribute the citrus oils, then discard.

SAN DOMINGUE

The funk and flavor of a great Jamaican dark rum, such as Appleton Estate 12 Year Rare Casks, makes an excellent base for a boozy drink. With the anise hit of Peychaud's bitters and a fruity banana liqueur rinse, this cocktail will play with your mind. Are you drinking a cocktail or an extremely nuanced rum?

2 ounces Jamaican dark rum

¼ ounce Raw Sugar Syrup (page 256)

3 dashes Peychaud's bitters

1 dash orange bitters

¼ ounce Giffard Banane du Bresil liqueur for rinsing (page 61)

1 orange peel for garnish

Chill a rocks glass in advance. In a mixing glass, combine all the ingredients except the Banane du Bresil and fill the mixing glass three-quarters full of ice. Rinse the chilled rocks glass with the Banane du Bresil. Stir the mixing glass for 30 seconds and strain into the prepared rocks glass. Express a 1-inch round of orange peel, skin side down, over the surface of the drink, run the skin around the rim of the glass to distribute the citrus oils, then discard.

DAUPHINE

Traditionalists will appreciate the dynamic flavors of this riff, which skews herbal and savory thanks to celery bitters and green Chartreuse. Like absinthe, green Chartreuse runs high in alcohol (55% ABV), making this a powerful drink indeed.

2 ounces rye whiskey

½ ounce Simple Syrup (page 255)

3 dashes Peychaud's bitters

1 dash celery bitters

¼ ounce green Chartreuse for rinsing

1 lemon peel for garnish

Chill a rocks glass in advance. In a mixing glass, combine all the ingredients except the Chartreuse and fill the mixing glass three-quarters full of ice. Rinse the chilled rocks glass with the Chartreuse. Stir the mixing glass for 30 seconds and strain into the prepared rocks glass. Express a 1-inch round of lemon peel, skin side down, over the surface of the drink, run the skin around the rim of the glass to distribute the citrus oils, then discard.

EVERY COCKTAIL HAS A TWIST

San Domingue

PALE FIRE

Not quite a dark spirit, barrel-aged gin nonetheless has weight and heft that its unaged brethren lack. We love Barr Hill Tom Cat Gin, made with a base of raw honey. This gin contributes beautiful botanicals to this clever Sazerac-esque cocktail, with a rinse of maraschino liqueur, a classic cherry liqueur from the Dulmatian coast. Confident and memorable.

1¼ ounces barrel-aged gin

½ ounce Pierre Ferrand Dry Curaçao

¼ ounce Honey Syrup (page 255)

3 dashes Peychaud's bitters

1 dash Angostura bitters

¼ ounce maraschino liqueur for rinsing

1 lemon peel for garnish

Chill a rocks glass in advance. In a mixing glass, combine all the ingredients except the maraschino liqueur and fill the mixing glass three-quarters full of ice. Rinse the chilled rocks glass with the maraschino liqueur. Stir the mixing glass for 30 seconds and strain into the prepared rocks glass. Express a 1-inch round of lemon peel, skin side down, over the surface of the drink, run the skin around the rim of the glass to distribute the citrus oils, then discard.

CATCH 22

We never knew we needed a Tequila Sazerac until this drink hit our lips. Yellow Chartreuse, absinthe, and Peychaud's bitters add layers atop the reposado's smooth base to incredible effect. The grapefruit twist has an aromatic but drying influence. Don't skip this one.

1½ ounces Tequila reposado

½ ounce yellow Chartreuse

¼ ounce Light Agave Syrup (page 255)

3 dashes Peychaud's bitters

1 dash grapefruit bitters

¼ ounce absinthe for rinsing

1 grapefruit peel for garnish

Chill a rocks glass in advance. In a mixing glass, combine all the ingredients except the absinthe and fill the mixing glass three-quarters full of ice. Rinse the chilled rocks glass with the absinthe. Stir the mixing glass for 30 seconds and strain into the prepared rocks glass. Express a 1-inch round of grapefruit peel, skin side down, over the surface of the drink, run the skin around the rim of the glass to distribute the citrus oils, then discard.

23.

SIDECARS

VINTAGE · SEXY · REFINED

I want my Sidecar . . .

It's a shame that more people don't know the Sidecar these days, so let's make a round, shall we? An elegant sour of Cognac, orange liqueur, and lemon juice, the Sidecar abounded in the 1920s—first in France, then America—but faded in popularity over the decades. Today it lacks the name recognition of a Manhattan or even a Negroni.

While beloved by bartenders, Cognac hasn't taken off in the United States as Bourbon or Tequila have. Price may be one factor because good Cognac doesn't come cheap. Familiarity may be another because most Americans don't keep a bottle at home, but it's worth investing in one. A masterpiece of aging and blending, good Cognac spends years, even *decades*, aging in the cask. Its elegance in cocktails is nearly unmatched.

That's why every cocktail lover should experience the glory of a perfectly shaken Sidecar. A potent spitfire, it smoothly disguises its high proof. The Sidecar can drink as strong as the Martini, it just doesn't let you know it. So despite its vibrancy, the Sidecar isn't a lighthearted party drink. Take your time with it and share it with someone special. Once you fall in love with this classic—and you will—we've got half a dozen more variations for you to try.

BUY THESE BOTTLES

You can find lots of brandies, including Cognacs, and inexpensive bottles are great for, say, spiking eggnog. But for a Sidecar, brandy commands center stage, so you want something more refined. Spring for H by Hine, a Cognac created explicitly for cocktails, as one excellent option. Courvoisier VSOP, which costs about the same, holds up beautifully in a cocktail, as well. Either will yield a drink rich in flavor and smooth and silky in texture. Cognac-style American brandies, such as Germain-Robin or Argonaut, also make great choices.

SUGAR RIM

Over the years, the Sidecar evolved a sugared rim, perhaps to mask the potency of the drink itself. It looks nice, but straight sugar doesn't contribute any flavor other than the obvious. Our solution? Sugars flavored with citrus zest. Orange zested sugar and lime-grapefruit zested sugar each contribute a different citrus element to the bright and lively drink.

OUR CLASSIC SIDECAR

Some recipes use equal parts cognac, orange liqueur, and lemon juice, but we think the drink tastes better balanced with double the cognac. We recommend using Cointreau for the orange liqueur here, which has the same ABV as the Cognac, so sip slowly.

2 ounces Cognac

1 ounce orange liqueur

1 ounce lemon juice

1 lemon peel for garnish

In a cocktail shaker, combine all the ingredients. Fill the shaker with ice and seal it. Shake vigorously for 15 seconds and double strain into a chilled coupe. Express a 3-inch strip of lemon peel, skin side down, over the surface of the drink, run the skin around the rim of the glass to distribute the citrus oils, and add the peel, skin side up, to the cocktail.

SOUTH AMERICAN SIDECAR

Both Peru and Chile claim themselves as the birthplace of Pisco, an unaged grape brandy. (Most good brands in America come from Peru.) You most likely will see it in a Pisco Sour. But here, it subs for Cognac, while grapefruit liqueur switches out for the orange liqueur. Think of it as a Sidecar with the fresh energy of the Margarita. Punchy citrus sugar adds to the appeal.

Lime and Grapefruit
   Sugar (page 261) to rim
   (optional)

1½ ounces Pisco

1 ounce pamplemousse
   liqueur

¼ ounce lemon juice

¼ ounce lime juice

1 lime wedge for garnish

If desired, rim a rocks glass with the lime and grapefruit. Set aside the prepared glass. In a cocktail shaker, combine all the ingredients. Fill the shaker with ice and seal it. Shake vigorously for 15 seconds and strain into the prepared glass filled with ice. Squeeze a lime wedge into the glass and drop it in.

IL CARROZZINO

Here, you'll bring all the flavors of a Sidecar into an elegant drink that's stirred, not shaken. Limoncello contributes sweetness and a bright burst of citrus. For this precisely balanced drink, we recommend Pierre Ferrand Dry Curaçao for the orange liqueur. No juicing required, but don't skip the lemon twist.

1½ ounces Cognac

¾ ounce orange liqueur

¾ ounce limoncello

2 dashes orange bitters

1 lemon peel for garnish

In a mixing glass, combine all the ingredients. Fill the mixing glass three-quarters full of ice. Stir for 30 seconds and strain into a chilled coupe. Express a 3-inch strip of lemon peel, skin side down, over the surface of the drink, run the skin around the rim of the glass to distribute the citrus oils, and add the peel, skin side up, to the cocktail.

SPEAKEASY SIDECAR

The Sidecar proper is one of the sneakily booziest drinks out there, so even a lighter version still drinks like a proper cocktail. Here, you'll split the Cognac with Lillet Blanc, which, together, make a seamless backdrop for aromatic Meyer lemon. Fragrant, dynamic, delicious.

1 ounce Cognac

1 ounce Lillet Blanc

1 ounce orange liqueur

¾ ounce Meyer lemon juice

¼ ounce lemon juice

1 Meyer lemon peel for
   garnish

In a cocktail shaker, combine all the ingredients. Fill the shaker with ice and seal it. Shake vigorously for 15 seconds and double strain into a chilled coupe. Express a 2–3-inch strip of Meyer lemon peel, skin side down, over the surface of the drink, run the skin around the rim of the glass to distribute the citrus oils, and add the peel, skin side up, to the cocktail.

SANGUINELLO

Blood orange imparts a dramatic color, which is reason enough to use it in a cocktail, but so is its distinctive flavor. It matches beautifully with the compelling, honeyed Amaro Nonino, creating one of the smoothest Sidecars you'll ever sip. If you can, use Cointreau as the orange liqueur here.

1 ounce Cognac

1 ounce blood orange juice

¾ ounce orange liqueur

¾ ounce Amaro Nonino

½ ounce lemon juice

1 lemon peel for garnish

1 blood orange slice for
  garnish

In a cocktail shaker, combine all the ingredients. Fill the shaker with ice and seal it. Shake vigorously for 15 seconds and strain into a rocks glass filled with ice. Express a 3-inch strip of lemon peel, skin side down, over the surface of the drink, run the skin around the rim of the glass to distribute the citrus oils, and add the peel, skin side up, to the cocktail. Also garnish with a half-moon slice of blood orange.

THE KING'S SIDECAR

The Sidecar has such power and clarity that you shouldn't muddy it with a ton of extraneous flavors. But the sharp bite of ginger suits it perfectly. Rather than using ginger juice, reach for The King's Ginger, a 40% ABV liqueur, which keeps the drink as strong and punchy as the original. If you can, use Cointreau as the orange liqueur, also 40% ABV.

1 ounce Cognac

1 ounce The King's Ginger

1 ounce orange liqueur

1 ounce lemon juice

1 dash orange bitters

1 lemon peel for garnish

In a cocktail shaker, combine all the ingredients. Fill the shaker with ice and seal it. Shake vigorously for 15 seconds and double strain into a chilled coupe. Express a 3-inch strip of lemon peel, skin side down, over the surface of the drink, run the skin around the rim of the glass to distribute the citrus oils, and add the peel, skin side up, to the cocktail.

EVERY COCKTAIL HAS A TWIST

PUTTING ON THE RITZ

Orange liqueur helps define a Sidecar. Here, you'll play with many citrus elements: orange-heavy Amaro Montenegro, Grand Marnier, orange and lemon juices, and an orange-zested sugar rim.

Orange Sugar (page 261) to rim (optional)

1 ounce Cognac

1 ounce Amaro Montenegro

1 ounce Grand Marnier

½ ounce lemon juice

½ ounce orange juice

1 orange peel for garnish

If desired, rim a chilled coupe with orange-zested sugar. Set aside the prepared glass. In a cocktail shaker, combine all the ingredients. Fill the shaker with ice and seal it. Shake vigorously for 15 seconds and double strain into the prepared glass. Express a 3–4-inch strip of orange peel, skin side down, over the surface of the drink, and add the peel, skin side up, to the cocktail.

APPLE OF MY EYE

One of Napoléon Bonaparte's brothers lived in New Jersey for a time, so let's think beyond France for brandy and go to the Garden State. While we're at it, let's hit Oregon for some pears. Each flavor contributes a vivid orchard element to a still recognizable Sidecar. If you can, use Pierre Ferrand Dry Curaçao for the orange liqueur.

1½ ounces Laird's Straight Apple Brandy Bottled in Bond 100

1 ounce orange liqueur

1 ounce lemon juice

½ ounce Clear Creek Pear Brandy

1 lemon peel for garnish

In a cocktail shaker, combine all the ingredients. Fill the shaker with ice and seal it. Shake vigorously for 15 seconds and double strain into a chilled coupe. Express a 3-inch strip of lemon peel, skin side down, over the surface of the drink, run the skin around the rim of the glass to distribute the citrus oils, and add the peel, skin side up, to the cocktail.

24.

TOM COLLINSES

SLEEK · UPLIFTING · EASYGOING

Let's make our Collins . . .

If you don't know Tom Collins, imagine a boozy, sparkling lemonade. With gin, lemon, sugar, and sparkling water, it's light, refreshing, and awfully likable. From the 1880s through the mid-1900s, the Tom Collins served as a bar staple known to all. Throughout the years, it proved so popular that its signature glass bears its name.

Different variations of this infinitely adaptable drink have become popular over time: the whiskey Collins, the vodka Collins. With white rum, it becomes a Pedro Collins; with Cognac, Pierre Collins; with Tequila, Juan Collins—you get the idea. Those are the classic iterations, but the variations don't stop at simply switching the spirit. Virtually any flavor can find its way into some kind of Collins: strawberry and vanilla, lime and coconut, shiso and sake, cucumber and aloe. The hardest part might be naming them all.

BUY THIS BOTTLE

A classic London dry gin, Beefeater makes a great choice for a Collins.

OUR CLASSIC TOM COLLINS

Gin really does make for a perfectly refreshing tall drink, but swap in vodka or any other spirit if you prefer.

1½ ounces gin

½ ounce lemon juice

½ ounce Simple Syrup
 (page 255)

2 ounces club soda

1 lemon wheel for garnish

In a cocktail shaker, combine all the ingredients except the club soda. Fill the shaker with ice and seal it. Shake vigorously for 15 seconds and strain into a Collins glass filled with ice. Top with the club soda and stir gently and briefly. Garnish with a lemon wheel.

Who's Tom Collins?

You reasonably might wonder, *Was there a real Tom Collins?* As is often the case with cocktail origin stories, the answer is . . . complicated.

Named for the owner of Limmer's Old House, a beloved and notoriously unruly tavern in early 19th-century London, the drink originated as the John Collins. The proprietor served a gin punch (gin, lemon, and sugar) as a long drink with sparkling water, and the Collins was born. John Collins, the drink, eventually crossed the Atlantic. Concurrently, the "Old Tom" style of gin, sweeter than the London dry style, had risen in popularity. Then a popular prank emerged stateside. Men warned one another that "Tom Collins" had been disparaging them in public, resulting in searches of bars and taverns to track down the scoundrel. In the era of social media, this lark probably would burn out within hours, but in the 1800s it proved surprisingly enduring. Newspapers of the time documented the joke, in New York City and Philadelphia in particular. People even wrote songs about the notorious Collins.

John Collins, Old Tom Gin, a Tom Collins joke—with all these names in the drinking zeitgeist, it remains unclear whether a single enterprising bartender first (re)named the Tom Collins, but by the end of the 1800s, Tom Collins had stuck. Old Tom Gin itself as the base for a Collins didn't, though. In later decades, as today, the Collins made use of London dry gin. No one ever said drinking made sense.

STRAWBERRY FIELDS

What could taste nicer on a summer day than this union of juicy strawberries and a quick vanilla syrup? We usually prefer gin in a Collins, but vodka plays a background role here to let the other flavors shine.

3 strawberries, hulled, plus ½ for garnish

1½ ounces vodka

¾ ounce Vanilla Syrup (page 256)

½ ounce lemon juice

2 ounces club soda

1 lemon wheel for garnish

In the bottom of a cocktail shaker, add the strawberries and muddle until they break up and release their juice. Add the remaining ingredients except the club soda. Fill the shaker with ice and seal it. Shake vigorously for 15 seconds and double strain into a Collins glass filled with ice. Top with the club soda and stir gently and briefly. Garnish with half a strawberry and a lemon wheel.

TRUDY COLLINS

One reason to love winter: It's citrus season. When life gives you blood oranges, juice 'em and make cocktails.

1½ ounces vodka

1 ounce blood orange juice

½ ounce lemon juice

½ ounce Simple Syrup (page 255)

10 leaves mint

2 ounces club soda

2 or 3 sprigs mint for garnish

1 blood orange slice for garnish

In a cocktail shaker, combine all the ingredients except the club soda. Fill the shaker with ice and seal it. Shake vigorously for 15 seconds and double strain into a Collins glass filled with ice. Top with the club soda and stir gently and briefly. Lightly tap the mint sprigs against your hand to release to release their fragrant oils before bundling them into a bouquet and adding them to the glass. Also garnish with a half-moon slice of blood orange.

TIP: Swap white rum for the vodka and lime juice for the lemon juice, and you'll make a mighty nice blood orange Mojito.

FAIR STREET

Cappelletti, a wine-based aperitif, brings down the proof of this Collins, while basil contributes a fragrant lift. Easy drinking enough for daytime, sophisticated enough for an evening cocktail party.

1 ounce gin

1 ounce Cappelletti

½ ounce lemon juice

¼ ounce Simple Syrup (page 255)

3 leaves basil, torn in half just before added to shaker, plus 1 sprig for garnish

2 ounces club soda

In a cocktail shaker, combine all the ingredients except the club soda. Fill the shaker with ice and seal it. Shake vigorously for 15 seconds and double strain into a Collins glass filled with ice. Top with the club soda and stir gently and briefly. Lightly tap a pretty basil sprig against your hand to release the aromatic oils before adding it to the drink.

Riffing on the Classics

Modern bartenders love to play with classic cocktails, using them as templates for experimentation. Bartenders in the past were just as prolific. Taking a popular drink and figuring out how to tweak it in every way possible has formed an integral part of mixology since time immemorial. David Embury's seminal book, *The Fine Art of Mixing Drinks* (1948), lists 12 Collinses by name and even includes a then little-known Mint Collins, the "Mojito," in their number.

SHISO-SAKE COLLINS

The basic backdrop of a Collins, citrus and soda, can function as a platform to highlight delicate flavors. Here, you'll pair fragrant shiso leaves with sake for a dry, refreshing cocktail with unusual subtlety (we recommend a junmai daiginjo sake). Shiso also happens to be one of the most effortlessly attractive garnishes you'll ever see.

1½ ounces sake

¾ ounce Tequila blanco

¾ ounce Simple Syrup (page 255)

½ ounce lemon juice

½ ounce lime juice

3 large leaves shiso, plus more for garnish

2 ounces club soda

In a cocktail shaker, combine all the ingredients except the club soda. Fill the shaker with ice and seal it. Shake vigorously for 15 seconds and strain into a Collins glass filled with ice. Top with the club soda and stir gently and briefly. Lightly tap a shiso leaf against your hand. Nestle it around the interior rim of the glass. If your shiso has a photogenic sprig, gently place it in front of the leaf.

LILY COLLINS

Reach for Lillet when you want sophisticated citrus flavor without too much alcohol. Coconut water lightens this drink still further. This rare-because-genuinely hydrating cocktail runs low in proof but big on personality.

2 ounces Lillet Rosé

2 ounces coconut water

½ ounce lemon juice

¼ ounce Simple Syrup (page 255)

1 ounce club soda

1 lime wedge for garnish

1 sprig mint for garnish

In a cocktail shaker, combine all the ingredients except the club soda. Fill the shaker with ice and seal it. Shake vigorously for 15 seconds and strain into a Collins glass filled with ice. Top with the club soda and stir gently and briefly. Squeeze a lime wedge into the glass and drop it in. Lightly tap a mint sprig against your hand to release the aromatic oils before adding it to the drink.

CUCUMBER COLLINS

One of the most appealing cocktail ingredients, fresh cucumber juice creates a cooling backdrop for lemon and gin. Aromatic aloe liqueur has a way of making any bright, spirited cocktail taste even better.

1 ounce gin

1 ounce Chareau Aloe
   Liqueur

1 ounce Cucumber Juice
   (page 260)

½ ounce lemon juice

½ ounce Simple Syrup
   (page 255)

1 ounce club soda

1 cucumber slice for garnish

In a cocktail shaker, combine all the ingredients except the club soda. Fill the shaker with ice and seal it. Shake vigorously for 15 seconds and strain into a Collins glass filled with ice. Top with the club soda and stir gently and briefly. Garnish with a long, thin, bias-cut slice of cucumber.

NOTE: Cucumber juice is easy to make in a juicer or blender (page 260), but it declines in quality rapidly. Use it the day you make it.

TIP: If you can't find Chareau, a simpler Cucumber Collins also tastes delicious. Prepare as described here, omitting the aloe liqueur, and up the gin to 1½ ounces and the club soda to 2 ounces.

BUY THIS BOTTLE

Chareau Aloe Liqueur

25.

WHISKEY SOURS

AFFABLE · RESTRAINED · UNDERAPPRECIATED

I'll have it . . .

Few if any other drinks are so foundational to modern mixology yet so little remembered. You probably have heard of the Whiskey Sour even if you've never ordered one by name. But from the late 1800s through the mid-1900s, the Whiskey Sour was an absolute staple, one of the most popular orders at any bar. Like the Gimlet, Daiquirí, and Margarita, it belongs to (surprise!) the sour family: spirit, citrus, sweetener.

For a Whiskey Sour, Bourbon, lemon juice, and sugar form the basic template. In the 1920s, the addition of egg white became standard, yielding a light, elegant drink with a fluffy white head. If you order a Whiskey Sour at an upscale bar today, you likely will receive the egg white version, which is considered a bit more old-fashioned, even though the simpler version has the longer history.

In recent years, the Whiskey Sour hasn't really had its own moment. It's not as in-demand as an Old-Fashioned, nor does it have the cachet of a French 75. But a number of craft cocktails, including modern classics such as the Penicillin (Scotch, lemon juice, honey syrup), qualify as Whiskey Sours even if menus don't call them that. Bourbon and citrus always taste damn good together. As you'll see and taste, the Whiskey Sour suits to any season, any occasion, any hour. Once you've learned the basics, any number of variations lie just a shake away.

OUR CLASSIC WHISKEY SOUR

Whiskey, lemon, sugar: punchy and delicious.

2 ounces Bourbon

1 ounce lemon juice

¾ ounce Simple Syrup
(page 255)

1 cocktail cherry for garnish

In a cocktail shaker, combine all the ingredients. Fill the shaker with ice and seal it. Shake vigorously for 15 seconds and strain into a rocks glass filled with ice. Garnish with a cocktail cherry.

UP OR ROCKS?

We generally prefer Whiskey Sours on the rocks with the exception of some egg white sours that benefit from the elegance of a coupe. But you can serve any of these Whiskey Sour drinks in a coupe if you like.

WHISKEY SOUR WITH EGG WHITE

Using egg whites imparts a smooth, silky texture that suits a sour perfectly.

1 medium egg white

2 ounces Bourbon

1 ounce lemon juice

¾ ounce Simple Syrup
(page 255)

1 orange slice for garnish

1 cocktail cherry for garnish

To a cocktail shaker, add the egg white and then the rest of the ingredients. Shake hard for 15 seconds. Open the shaker, add ice, and shake again for 15 seconds. Strain into a rocks glass filled with ice and garnish with a half-moon slice of orange and a cocktail cherry.

Why Egg White?

Raw egg whites, by themselves, aren't appealing, but they play an important role in the history of some cocktails, none more so than the Whiskey Sour. (They also play starring roles in the Silver Gin Fizz and Pisco Sour.)

Egg whites don't contribute much in the way of flavor; they don't make a drink taste "eggy," for example. They also don't make a drink heavy, the way a whole egg will. Egg white is all about texture. They give a cocktail a light, silky body. Imagine them as a blank canvas on which delicate flavors can emerge. When cooking, butter can mellow but not mask the acidity of lemon or vinegar. Egg white has a similar effect. It also creates a gorgeous foam head, which gives a drink immediate elegance. (While pasturized, egg whites from a carton will do in a pinch—and aquafaba, the leftover liquid from canned chickpeas, is a viable vegan substitute—both create a slightly looser foam that's not quite the same as a fresh egg white.)

Common-sense rules apply when working with raw eggs. Use fresh eggs and discard if they look or smell off. A good tip: When a drink calls for egg white, add it to your shaker first. That way, if you accidentally get some yolk or shell in there, you can remove it (or start over) without wasting any booze.

Shaking drinks with egg whites requires an extra step, what bartenders call the double shake. Combine all the ingredients in your shaker *without* ice, seal it, and shake to emulsify. Then open the shaker, add ice, and shake again to chill and dilute.

Some professional bartenders keep a squeeze bottle of egg whites at their work stations, measuring them by the ounce or half-ounce. Although that approach makes sense for high-volume bars, it's impractical for making drinks at home, where you'd need to maneuver an egg white from shell to jigger. So we'll skip exact measurements for egg whites in these recipes. One small-to-medium egg white, approximately 1 ounce, works for just about any sour.

For punchy and tart sours that go bolder on the lemon, skip the egg white. For more delicate flavors and a softer effect overall, use an egg white. You can make any of these drinks with or without it. If you omit it, expect the citrus and spirit flavors to taste more dominant.

IRISH ROSE

You don't need to overthink some drinks—simple and perfect.

1 medium egg white

1½ ounces Irish whiskey

¾ ounce lemon juice

¾ ounce Raspberry Syrup (page 257)

1 dash orange bitters

1 orange peel for garnish

1 raspberry for garnish

To a cocktail shaker, add the egg white and then the rest of the ingredients. Shake hard for 15 seconds. Open the shaker, add ice, and shake again for 15 seconds. Double strain into a chilled coupe. Express a 3–4-inch strip of orange peel, skin side down, over the surface of the drink, run the skin around the rim of the glass to distribute the citrus oils, and add the peel, skin side up, to the cocktail. Also garnish with a raspberry on a cocktail pick.

IF I HAD A HAMMER

On many a back bar but not always appreciated properly, Drambuie combines aged Scotch, heathered honey, and herbs. This recipe amplifies the Scotch and honey notes, with a hint of cinnamon, in a surprisingly delicate sour. No need to pull out a pricey bottle of Scotch here. Use a less expensive blend such as Famous Grouse or Bank Note.

1 medium egg white

1½ ounces blended Scotch

¾ ounce Drambuie

¾ ounce lemon juice

¾ ounce Cinnamon Honey Syrup (page 256)

1 stick cinnamon for garnish

1 cocktail cherry for garnish

To a cocktail shaker, add the egg white and then the rest of the ingredients. Shake hard for 15 seconds. Open the shaker, add ice, and shake again for 15 seconds. Strain into rocks glass filled with ice. Garnish with a long cinnamon stick and a cocktail cherry.

ALAMEDA SOUR

The New York Sour is simply a Whiskey Sour with a red wine float. This recipe ups the usual amount of wine and takes it in a mulled direction. St. George Spiced Pear Liqueur tastes like an autumn fantasy in a bottle, all orchard flavors and warm spice. It nestles in here, cozy as anything. For the wine, go big and jammy with a Zinfandel or Malbec.

1 medium egg white

1½ ounces Bourbon or rye

1 ounce St. George Spiced Pear Liqueur (page 118)

¾ ounce lemon juice

¾ ounce Simple Syrup (page 255)

1 ounce red wine

To a cocktail shaker, add the egg white and then the rest of the ingredients, except the red wine. Shake hard for 15 seconds. Open the shaker, add ice, and shake again for 15 seconds. Strain into a large rocks glass filled with ice. Float the red wine on top by placing a barspoon just on the surface of the liquid and slowly pouring the wine into the barspoon to create a layer.

STIRRED SOUR

Can you really have a sour with no juice? Well, with the vivid citrus flavor of limon-cello, sure. Stir it with Bourbon, and you have something special.

2 ounces Bourbon or rye

1 ounce limoncello

½ ounce Simple Syrup (page 255)

1 lemon peel for garnish

1 cocktail cherry for garnish

In a mixing glass, combine all the ingredients. Fill the mixing glass three-quarters full of ice. Stir for 30 seconds and strain into a chilled coupe. Express a 3-inch strip of lemon peel, skin side down, over the surface of the drink, run the skin around the rim of the glass to distribute the citrus oils, and add the peel, skin side up, to the cocktail. Garnish with a cocktail cherry on a cocktail pick.

TANGERINE DREAM

If a Creamsicle became a sophisticated cocktail, this would be it. Fresh tangerine juice and a quick vanilla syrup give this drink a cheery, familiar flavor without going overboard on the sugar. Childhood vibe, adult drink.

1½ ounces Bourbon

¾ ounce tangerine juice

½ ounce Vanilla Syrup
(page 256)

¼ ounce lemon juice

1 lemon peel for garnish

1 segment tangerine for
garnish

In a cocktail shaker, combine all the ingredients. Fill the shaker with ice and seal it. Shake vigorously for 15 seconds and strain into a rocks glass filled with ice. Express a 3-inch strip of lemon peel, skin side down, over the surface of the drink, run the skin around the rim of the glass to distribute the citrus oils, and add the peel, skin side up, to the cocktail. Garnish with a tangerine segment.

ITALIAN GENTLEMAN

Campari isn't just for Negronis. Its bittersweetness works in so many cocktails, the Whiskey Sour among them. Not too bitter, not too tart—one of those drinks that comes together perfectly.

1½ ounces Bourbon

¾ ounce Campari

¾ ounce lemon juice

½ ounce Simple Syrup
(page 255)

2 dashes orange bitters

1 lemon peel for garnish

In a cocktail shaker, combine all the ingredients. Fill the shaker with ice and seal it. Shake vigorously for 15 seconds and strain into a rocks glass filled with ice. Express a 1-inch round of lemon peel, skin side down, over the surface of the drink, run the skin around the rim of the glass to distribute the citrus oils, and add the peel, skin side up, to the cocktail.

For 6 drinks, combine 9 ounces Bourbon, 4½ ounces Campari, 4½ ounces lemon juice, 3 ounces simple syrup, 12 dashes orange bitters, and 6 ounces of water in a quart container with a watertight lid. Refrigerate until ready to use. To serve, shake the container hard to combine the ingredients. Divide equally among six rocks glasses filled with ice, about 4½ ounces per glass, and garnish each with a lemon peel.

A LONG DECEMBER

Your next holiday party drink, sorted. Cranberry and rosemary honey give this drink a festive feel, friendly and winter ready. The rosy color and cheery garnish add to the appeal.

1½ ounces Bourbon

1 ounce Rosemary Honey (page 256)

¾ ounce 100% cranberry juice

¼ ounce lemon juice

2 dashes orange bitters

1 lemon wheel for garnish

1 sprig rosemary for garnish

In a cocktail shaker, combine all the ingredients. Fill the shaker with ice and seal it. Shake vigorously for 15 seconds and strain into a rocks glass filled with ice. Garnish with a thin lemon wheel. Firmly clap a rosemary sprig between your hands before adding it to the drink. Also garnish with a thin lemon wheel

NOTE: Use 100% cranberry juice, just cranberries and water listed as ingredients on the label. You need its pure tartness to balance the deliciously sweet rosemary honey.

BATCH IT

For 6 drinks, combine 9 ounces Bourbon, 6 ounces rosemary honey, 4½ ounces 100% cranberry juice, 1½ ounces lemon juice, 12 dashes orange bitters, and 6 ounces of water in a quart container with a watertight lid. Refrigerate until ready to use. To serve, shake the container hard to combine the ingredients. Divide equally among six rocks glasses filled with ice, about 4½ ounces per glass, and garnish each with a lemon wheel and rosemary sprig. If you want to serve the batch from a pitcher, try lightening it with 6 ounces of club soda.

SWEET TEA SOUR

You'll find the pure taste of a southern summer day right here: peaches, mint, sweet tea, and Bourbon, of course. Real sweet tea is too diluted to work as a good cocktail base, so use a sweet tea syrup with summery peach-infused bourbon. Get the rocking chairs on the front porch ready.

2 ounces Peach-Infused
    Bourbon (page 261)

1 ounce lemon juice

¾ ounce Sweet Tea Syrup
    (page 257)

2 dashes Angostura bitters

1 cocktail cherry for garnish

1 orange slice for garnish

3 sprigs mint for garnish

In a cocktail shaker, combine all the ingredients. Fill the shaker with ice and seal it. Shake vigorously for 15 seconds and strain into a rocks glass filled with ice. Garnish with a cocktail cherry and a thin half-moon slice of orange. Lightly tap the mint sprigs against your hand to release their aromatic oils before adding them to the drink.

For 6 drinks, combine 12 ounces peach-infused bourbon, 6 ounces lemon juice, 4½ ounces sweet tea syrup, 12 ounces Angostura bitters, and 6 ounces water in a quart container with a watertight lid. Refrigerate until ready to serve.

To serve, shake the container hard to combine the ingredients. Divide equally among 6 rocks glasses filled with ice and garnish as above.

APPENDIX

Syrups, Juices, Infusions, Sugars & Salts

SYRUPS

Making cocktail syrups requires a little preparation, but syrups offer one of the easiest, most efficient ways to introduce certain flavors in your drinks. Cinnamon offers a perfect example. Ground cinnamon would make a cocktail gritty. In anything other than a hot drink, a cinnamon stick garnish looks pretty but doesn't contribute much else. But a quick cinnamon syrup harnesses the spice's flavor perfectly.

The general method for making a syrup couldn't be more straightforward. Pour hot water over the starring ingredient, let it steep, stir in the sweetener, done. In the fridge, the syrup will keep for at least a week, ready for the moment you want to mix up a drink. Syrups also prove ideal to use in party drinks—such as the Raspberry Daiquirí (page 56) or the Strawberry Rhubarb Margarita (page 130)—because, once you've made the syrup, you've done most of the work already.

Simple Syrup

4 ounces water

4 ounces granulated white sugar

In a kettle or microwave, heat the water until nearly boiling. Add the sugar and stir until it dissolves completely. Let cool to room temperature before using. Makes approximately 7 ounces.

Honey Syrup

4 ounces water

4 ounces honey

In a kettle or microwave, heat the water until nearly boiling. Add the honey and stir until it dissolves completely. Let cool to room temperature before using. Makes 8 ounces.

Light Agave Syrup

4 ounces water

4 ounces light agave nectar

In a kettle or microwave, heat the water until nearly boiling. Add the agave nectar and stir until it dissolves completely. Let cool to room temperature before using. Makes 8 ounces.

Dark Agave Syrup

4 ounces water

4 ounces dark agave nectar

In a kettle or microwave, heat the water until nearly boiling. Add the agave nectar and stir until it dissolves completely. Let cool to room temperature before using. Makes 8 ounces.

Raw Sugar Syrup

4 ounces water

4 ounces raw sugar

In a kettle or microwave, heat the water until nearly boiling. Add the sugar and stir until it dissolves completely. Raw sugar needs more time to dissolve than granulated sugar. If it's taking a while, reheat it and resume stirring. Let cool to room temperature before using. Makes approximately 7 ounces.

Vanilla Syrup

4 ounces water

½ vanilla bean, halved lengthwise

4 ounces granulated white sugar

In a kettle or microwave, heat the water until nearly boiling. In a sealable container, add the hot water and vanilla. Steep for 20 minutes, add the sugar, and stir until it dissolves completely. Cover and let sit overnight or at least 8 hours. Strain the vanilla out before using. Makes approximately 7 ounces.

Rosemary Honey

4 ounces water

5 large sprigs rosemary (5 inches long)

4 ounces honey

In a kettle or microwave, heat the water until nearly boiling. In a sealable container, add the hot water and rosemary. Steep for 20 minutes, add the honey, and stir until it dissolves completely. Let steep until completely cool, about 1 hour. Strain before using. Makes approximately 8 ounces.

Cinnamon Syrup

1 cup water

5 sticks cinnamon (3 inches long)

1 cup granulated white sugar

In a kettle or microwave, heat the water until nearly boiling. In a sealable container, add the hot water and cinnamon sticks. Steep for 20 minutes, add the sugar, and stir until it dissolves completely. Steep overnight in the refrigerator and remove the cinnamon sticks before using. Makes approximately 14 ounces.

Cinnamon Honey Syrup

1 cup water

5 sticks cinnamon (3 inches long)

1 cup honey

In a kettle or microwave, heat the water until nearly boiling. In a sealable container, add the hot water and cinnamon sticks. Steep for 20 minutes, add the honey, and stir until it dissolves completely. Steep overnight in the refrigerator and remove the cinnamon sticks before using. Makes 16 ounces.

Sweet Tea Syrup

4 ounces water

1 teabag black tea of choice

4 ounces granulated white sugar

In a kettle or microwave, heat the water until nearly boiling. In a sealable container, add the hot water and tea bag. Steep for 10 minutes. Remove the tea bag, pressing to extract excess liquid. Add the sugar and stir until it dissolves completely. Makes approximately 7 ounces.

Mint Syrup

For this recipe, you want roughly half a bunch of mint, about 15 to 18 grams. Keep the leaves on the stems initially. Blanching keeps the syrup green and prevents it from developing oxidized flavors.

½ cup water

4 ounces granulated white sugar

½ bunch fresh mint

First, make simple syrup. In a kettle or microwave, heat ½ cup of the water until nearly boiling. Add the sugar and stir until it dissolves completely. Set aside. Boil a small pot of water. Blanch the mint sprigs for 15 seconds, then plunge them into ice water. Remove them, once cool, and pat dry with towel. Pick off the leaves and add them to a blender. Add the simple syrup and blend until smooth, 30 seconds or more. Strain through a fine mesh strainer, pressing gently to extract all the liquid. Discard the solids. Makes approximately 11 ounces.

Mint Tea Syrup

1 cup water

2 tea bags mint tea

1 cup granulated white sugar

In a kettle or microwave, heat the water until nearly boiling. In a sealable container, add the hot water and tea bags. Steep for 10 minutes. Remove the tea bags, pressing to extract all the liquid. Add the sugar and stir until it dissolves completely. Let cool to room temperature before using. Makes approximately 16 ounces.

Raspberry Syrup

6 ounces raspberries

1 cup granulated white sugar

4 ounces water

In a metal bowl, use the back of a spoon to smash the raspberries. Add the sugar and mix to form a paste. Let macerate for 20 minutes. In a kettle or microwave, heat the water until nearly boiling. Add the hot water to the raspberry mixture and stir until the sugar dissolves. Strain through a fine mesh strainer, pressing gently to extract all the liquid, and discard the solids. Makes approximately 11 ounces.

Strawberry Rhubarb Blender Syrup

4 ounces Simple Syrup (page 255)

3 rhubarb segments (approximately 6 inches long, 200g), roughly chopped

8 medium strawberries, hulled and halved (approximately 100g)

Into a blender, pour the simple syrup followed by the rhubarb and strawberries. Blend on low speed, then high, until smooth. Pour through a fine mesh strainer and use the back of a spoon to press the mixture through the mesh. Discard the solids. Use right away or cover and refrigerate. Makes approximately 10 ounces.

Hibiscus Syrup

6 ounces water

2 tea bags Tazo Passion Herbal Tea

6 ounces granulated white sugar

In a kettle or microwave, heat the water until nearly boiling. In a sealable container, add the hot water and the tea bags. Steep for 10 minutes. Remove the tea bags, pressing them to extract all the liquid. Add the sugar and stir until it dissolves completely. Let cool to room temperature before using. Makes approximately 10 ounces.

Orgeat

100g whole almonds (approximately ⅔ cup)

300g hot water (approximately 1¼ cups)

Granulated white sugar (measurement varies, see below)

½ teaspoon orange flower water

⅛ teaspoon salt

Roughly crush the almonds. In a small pan over high heat, toast the almond pieces until fragrant and lightly brown, shaking often, about 2 to 3 minutes. Into a blender, add the toasted almond pieces and the hot water. Blend on high until smooth. Strain the mixture through cheesecloth or a nut milk bag, discarding the solids. Measure the almond milk by weight, wash out the blender, and return the almond milk to the cleaned blender. Add an equal weight of sugar (for 150g almond milk, add 150g sugar), orange flower water, and salt. Blend again to combine. Some separation may occur; if so, shake to recombine before using. Makes approximately 12 ounces.

Pecan Orgeat

50g whole pecans (approximately ½ cup)

150g hot water (approximately ⅔ cup)

Granulated white sugar (measurement varies, see below)

⅛ teaspoon orange flower water

⅛ teaspoon salt

Roughly crush the pecans. In a small pan over high heat, toast the pecans until fragrant and lightly brown, shaking often, about 2 to 3 minutes. Into a blender, add the toasted pecan pieces and the hot water. Blend on high until smooth. Strain the mixture through cheesecloth or a nut milk bag, discarding the solids. Measure the pecan milk by weight, wash out the blender, and return the pecan milk to the cleaned blender. Add an equal weight of sugar (for 75g pecan milk, add 75g sugar), orange flower water, and salt. Blend again to combine. Some separation may occur; if so, shake to recombine before using. Makes approximately 5 to 6 ounces.

Macadamia Orgeat

100g whole macadamia nuts (approximately ⅔ cup)

300g hot water (approximately 1⅓ cups)

Granulated white sugar (measurement varies, see below)

½ teaspoon orange flower water

⅛ teaspoon salt

Roughly crush the macadamia nuts. In a small pan over high heat, toast the macadamia nuts until fragrant and lightly brown, shaking often, about 2 to 3 minutes. Into a blender, add the toasted macadamia pieces and the hot water. Blend on high until smooth. Strain the mixture through cheesecloth or a nut milk bag, discarding the solids. Measure the macadamia milk by weight, wash out the blender, and return the macadamia milk to the cleaned blender. Add an equal weight of sugar (for 125g macadamia milk, add 125g sugar), orange flower water, and salt. Blend again to combine. Some separation may occur; if so, shake to recombine before using. Makes approximately 16 ounces.

Thai Lime–Lemongrass Oleo Saccharum

8 medium limes (approximately 130g)

1 cup granulated white sugar

4 ounces water

6 lemongrass stalks, outer layer and dry ends removed (approximately 60g), thinly sliced

2 Thai lime leaves, thinly sliced

With a Y-shaped vegetable peeler, peel the limes, preserving as much green skin and avoiding as much white pith as possible. (Reserve the peeled limes for juice for another recipe.) In a sealable container, add the lime peels and sugar. Seal and shake well so the sugar fully covers the peels. Allow to emulsify overnight. (The citrus oils and sugar will start to form a liquid.)

In a kettle or microwave, heat the water until nearly boiling. In a sealable container, add the hot water, lemongrass, and Thai lime leaves. Steep for 20 minutes, strain, gently pressing the lemongrass to extract all the liquid, and discard the solids. Microwave the liquid for 1 minute or heat it on the stovetop until nearly boiling. Pour the heated liquid into the peel-sugar mix and stir until the sugar dissolves fully. Strain and discard the peels. Makes approximately 12 ounces.

Orange Oleo Saccharum

1 orange

1 ounce water

¼ cup granulated white sugar

With a Y-shaped vegetable peeler, peel the orange, preserving as much orange skin and avoiding as much white pith as possible. (Reserve the rest of the fruit for the Sangria Española.) In a sealable container, add the orange peels and sugar. Seal and shake well so the sugar fully covers the peels. Allow to emulsify overnight. (The citrus oils and sugar will start to form a liquid.) Shake again, uncover, and add 1 ounce hot water to the peel-sugar mix. Stir until the sugar dissolves fully. Makes a little more than 2 ounces.

Grenadine

1 orange

1 cup 100% pomegranate juice

1 cup granulated white sugar

1 stick cinnamon (approximately 3 inches long)

½ teaspoon allspice berries

1 clove

With a Y-shaped vegetable peeler, peel the orange, preserving as much skin and avoiding as much white pith as possible. (Reserve the peeled orange for juice for another recipe.) In in a medium saucepan over medium-high heat, combine all the ingredients, bring to a boil, stirring until the sugar dissolves completely. Reduce heat to medium-low and simmer for 8 minutes. Remove from heat, let cool

to room temperature, and refrigerate, covered, overnight. Strain before using. Makes approximately 12 ounces.

JUICES

Use a hand juicer or countertop juice press to make all citrus juices, a juice extractor or blender for everything else.

Ginger Juice

Peel the ginger. Use a juice extractor to process ginger. Strain through a fine mesh strainer, discarding the fibers/solids.

Alternatively, cut peeled ginger into chunks, add to a blender, and add just enough water to cover the blades (approximately ¼ cup). Blend on high until smooth. Strain through a fine-mesh strainer, discarding the solids.

Cucumber Juice

Use a juice extractor to process the cucumber (skin on, to retain its vibrant green color). Alternately, cut the cucumber into chunks, add to a blender, and add just enough water to cover the blades (approximately ¼ cup). Blend on high until smooth. Strain through a fine-mesh strainer, gently pressing to extract all the liquid. Discard the solids.

Sugar Snap Pea Juice

Use a juice extractor to process peas. Strain through a fine mesh strainer, discarding the solids. 1 cup of sugar snap peas yields approximately 2 ounces.

INFUSIONS

Serrano-Infused Tequila

2 serrano chiles

One 750ml bottle tequila blanco

Quarter the serrano chiles lengthwise and destem them. Add, seeds included, to the bottle of tequila. Steep overnight, strain out the chiles and seeds, and funnel back into the bottle.

Horseradish–Infused Vodka

8 ounces vodka

10 grams peeled horseradish, thinly sliced

In a sealable container, combine the horseradish and vodka. Steep in the refrigerator for 24 hours. Strain out horseradish before using.

Blue Cheese and Dill–Infused Vodka

40g crumbled blue cheese

4g fresh dill

8 ounces vodka

In a sealable container, combine the blue cheese, dill, and vodka. Steep in the refrigerator for 24 hours. Strain through cheesecloth, discarding the solids.

Peach-Infused Bourbon

1 medium peach, pitted and sliced

8 ounces Bourbon

Into a sealable container, add the peach and Bourbon and cover. Steep overnight and strain before using. For a full bottle, infuse 3 peaches in one 750ml-bottle Bourbon. Mix the Bourbon-soaked peach bits with ice cream or in a fruit salad.

SUGARS AND SALTS

Lime and Grapefruit Sugar

1 teaspoon lime zest

½ teaspoon grapefruit zest

3 tablespoons granulated white sugar

Stir together until well mixed.

Orange Sugar

1 teaspoon orange zest

6 tablespoons granulated white sugar

Stir together until well mixed.

Grapefruit Salt

1 teaspoon grapefruit zest

4 teaspoons kosher salt

Stir together until well mixed.

Lime Salt

1 teaspoon lime zest

4 teaspoons kosher salt

Stir together until well mixed.

ACKNOWLEDGMENTS

First and foremost, we want to extend thanks to you for picking up this book, taking a look, and, hopefully, mixing a few drinks. Creating it was a labor of love, and we're excited about every single cocktail in here.

We feel incredibly lucky that such a great team supported this work: first and foremost, our powerhouse editors, Ann Treistman and James Jayo. Thanks as always to Vicky Bijur, a tireless advocate, thoughtful sounding board and first-class agent.

Collaborating with other creative minds is one of the joys of our profession, and photographer Rachel Weill and stylist Liz Lavoie lent their incredible talents to this book. Our cocktails have never looked more beautiful!

Thanks to our many friends and family who suggested cocktail ideas, or a name for a drink (turns out that you can run out of ideas for drink names around cocktail #150 or so). Special thanks to Debbie Siegel, who we quite literally could not have written this book without.

And finally, thanks to everyone who's made a recipe from this book, or our previous work, *Be Your Own Bartender*. Nothing makes us happier than hearing you've tried out a drink and liked it. Cheers!

INDEX